REV. FRANCIS R. DAVIS
ST. MARY'S CHURCH
40 Elizabeth St.
Dansville, NY 14437

TO INSURE PEACE ACKNOWLEDGE GOD

By
John Cardinal Krol,
Archbishop of Philadelphia

ST. PAUL EDITIONS

Library of Congress Cataloging in Publication Data
Krol, John Joseph, 1910-
  To insure peace acknowledge God.

  1. Sociology, Christian (Catholic) — Addresses, essays, lectures.   I.   Title.
BX1753.K76   261   78-12341

Copyright © 1978, by the Daughters of St. Paul

Printed in the U.S.A. by the Daughters of St. Paul
50 St. Paul's Ave., Jamaica Plain, Boston, Ma. 02130

The Daughters of St. Paul are an international religious congregation serving the Church with the communications media.

FOREWORD

The Apostolic Exhortation *On Evangelization* emphasizes the fact that the essential content—the foundation, the center and the summit—of the dynamism of evangelization is that sanctification and salvation are offered to all men in Christ Jesus. This salvation, which is transcendent, has its beginning in this life and its fulfillment in eternity. Since man is not an abstract being and the plan of creation is associated with the plan of Redemption, our evangelization must seek to convert, solely through the divine power of the message, both the personal and the collective consciences of the people as well as the activities in which they engage.

When the Daughters of St. Paul prevailed upon me to release to them copies of some of my homilies, talks, letters and invocations, they classified them under three broad headings. The first volume, *God—the Cornerstone of Our Life*, emphasizes the essential content of evangelization. This second volume, *To Insure Peace Acknowledge God*, addresses itself to the collective consciences and the activities of the People of God. The third volume is entitled *The Church—for Life-Giving Union with Christ*.

It is my fervent hope that this second volume as well as the first will in some modest way reflect the importance I attach to my role as a servant of the Gospel, and help my co-workers to appreciate their own opportunities as heralds of the Gospel.

CONTENTS

International Relations 13
(Address at the NCCW Painesville Deanery, Annual Diocesan Luncheon, on May 2, 1957.)
Social-religious approach — Peace demands a plan based on sane realism — Problem of man is basic — The nation — Patriotism — Patriotism and peace — The religious approach to peace

The Responsibility of Journalists to God and Society 22
(Address at the Convention of the Religious Newswriters Association, on June 24, 1957.)
Need for reaffirmation of basic concepts — Interpreting the First Amendment — Guiding public opinion in the path of truth and light

God — the Source of Human Rights and Liberty 34
(Address at the 76th Meeting Supreme Council Knights of Columbus States Dinner, on August 19, 1958.)
Man — a social creature — A true patriot — God — source of inalienable rights — Academic freedom — Freedom of speech — Freedom for religion

A Return to Complete Truth 43
(Address at the Dinner Meeting of the Ohio Prosecutors Association, on March 4, 1960.)
Legal learning and philosophy — A thorough grasp of certain philosophical principles — Various schools of philosophy — Natural law jurisprudence — Positive law jurisprudence — A return to natural law jurisprudence

The Church in Defense of Man's Dignity 52
> *(Address at the Diocesan Council of Catholic Youth, 9th Annual Convention, May 1, 1960.)*
> Affirming the individual — The right to liberty and to life — The Church's defense in word and in deed

The Substance of Your Profession — Justice and Love 59
> *(Address to the St. Thomas More Society of Philadelphia, on September 17, 1961.)*
> Religion — the parent of law — The jurist's vision

The Nation of Immigrants 65
> *(Address at a banquet of the American Committee on Italian Migration, on January 7, 1962.)*
> The basic human right to migrate — Migration brings social peace

Immigration — a Matter of Natural and Positive Law 72
> *(Address at the Third Annual Greater Philadelphia Conference on American Immigration Policy, Citizenship, and Refugee Matters, on December 15, 1964.)*
> Part of our national interest — Let the law reflect the heart of America — Immigration — a matter of law — Immigration — a matter of people

Neither Apathy, nor Indifference, nor Complacency, but Action 80
> *(Address at the Christian Weekend Retreat, on January 24, 1965.)*
> Christian action — The hour of charity — Poverty and prejudice

No Cultural Uniformity, but Political Unity 88
> *(Address at the 28th Biennial Convention*

of the Grand Lodge of Pennsylvania of the Order of the Sons of Italy in America, on June 26, 1965.)

Certain sociological movements — Theory of total assimilation — Principle of integration of cultures

The Duty of Government—To Promote and Protect the Rights of Men 97
(Sermon for the 7th Annual Observance of Sts. Cyril and Methodius Heritage Day, on July 13, 1969.)

Apostles of many Slavic peoples — A service of prayer for a just and lasting peace — Religious freedom — We pray for victims of militant atheism — Militant atheism has not—will not—cannot succeed — Violent suppression of freedom

Peace—an Enterprise of Justice Among Nations 106
(Address at the Memorial Service of the National Convention of Veterans of Foreign Wars, on August 17, 1969.)

Peace is not pacifism — The arms race — Directing all efforts towards peace

To Insure Peace Man Must Acknowledge God 116
(Acceptance of the 25th Anniversary Gold Medal Public Service Award from the Philadelphia Public Relations Association, on May 27, 1970.)

Need for a spiritual influence — Peace demands courage — God and His blueprint

The Church and Arms Limitation 124
(Excerpt from the talk delivered to the Synod in Rome, on October 22, 1971.)

Religion—Essential to a True and Lasting Peace 126

(Sermon at the White House, on December 17, 1972.)
Invitation to prayer — "Immanuel — God with us" — A message of love — Acknowledging God's authority, love and will — Final blessing

Statement on Abortion 136
(Issued from Washington, NCCB, January 22, 1973.)

United Against Godless Ideologies 138
(Presentation at the Colloquium on the Holocaust, on April 11, 1973.)
What is Nihilism? — National Socialism — Hitlerian Anti-Semitism — Lessons derived from the Holocaust — Jewish legacy to humankind

A Timely Instrument to Communicate Timeless Truth 152
(Statement on NC News Service Wire Transmission, on May 14, 1973.)

Demanding an End to Death-by-Abortion ... 155
(Letter to the faithful of the Archdiocese of Philadelphia, read at all Masses on January 20, 1974.)

Rededicating Ourselves to Protecting Life ... 160
(Comments at the Pro-Life Demonstration at Independence Hall Federal Court House, on January 22, 1974.)

Morality, Law and War in a Nuclear Age 162
(Address at the International Laws and Warfare Symposium, June 19-20, 1974.)
Moral argument — instrument of criticism and source of wisdom — The Vietnam experience — Search for peace in the nuclear age

A Work on Behalf of All People 170
(Address at the Annual Meeting Dinner of

the Pennsylvania Catholic Conference, on August 6, 1974.)

The ecclesiastical and civil powers — The ruling authority — A false concept of civil power — Inscribing the divine law in the earthly city

Deep Concern for the Lives of the Unborn ... 177
(Statement on the vote of the State Legislature to override the Shapp Veto of Abortion Bill 1318, on September 11, 1974.)

Human Rights and Reconciliation 179
(Statement of the Synod—1974, presented by John Cardinal Krol, on October 23, 1974.)
His Holiness, Pope Paul VI's comment on the document on Human Rights *(To the faithful in St. Peter's Square on October 27, 1974.)*

The Food Crisis 186
(At the Symposium on "Hunger and the American Conscience," on February 11, 1975.)
Crisis of civilization and of solidarity — Dimensions of the crisis — Areas of chronic famine — Shrinking grain reserves — The United States and the food crisis — The Church and the food crisis — The possibility of a solution

On the Guilty Verdict Rendered in the Abortion-Related Case in Boston 198
(Statement of February 15, 1975.)

We Must Live as a Family 199
(At the Dinner Reception in his honor in Cairo, Holy Year, 1975.)

Need for a Rebirth of Discipline and Morality 202
(Homily at St. Mary's Church, Philadelphia, on July 4, 1976, at the Bicentennial Liturgy of Thanksgiving and "Te Deum.")

St. Mary's and the Founding Fathers — E Pluribus Unum — Catholic unity — Declaration of Independence — a declaration of dependence on God — American and French Revolutions — We are a religious people — America is great because America is good — Corrective criticism — Concerns about certain trends

We Pray that America Will Return to Its Spiritual Foundations 218
(Broadcast on WFIL Radio, on December 27, 1976, December 31, 1976.)

Protecting Human Rights Everywhere in the World 220
(Homily at the Mass at the Sixth Annual Polish Festival, on June 5, 1977.)
Deep appreciation of human rights — Taking to heart the establishment of greater justice — Atheism vs. belief in God — Hunger for God

Attending to the Pastoral Needs of Immigrants 231
(Address, "Del Primer Encuentro Nacional Hispano de Pastoral al Segundo Encuentro," on August 19, 1977.)
The Church's solicitude for migrants — "A teeming nation of nations" — The Church of immigrants

Setting a Pro-Life Trend in Our Society 242
(Letter read at all Masses on Respect Life Sunday, October 2, 1977.)

On the Panama Canal Treaties 245
(Statement on behalf of the United States Catholic Conference, Washington, D.C., accompanied by Rev. J. Bryan Hehir, Director, Office of International Justice

and Peace, United States Catholic Conference, Washington, D.C., on October 10-14, 1977.)

Catholic bishops' interest in need for new treaty — Requirement of justice and peace — Symbolic significance of moment — Symbolic significance of treaties — Argument that United States will appear weak

Resolutely Safeguarding Human Life 255
(Keynote address at the Respect Life Educational Workshop, April 27, 1978.)

Pastoral plan for pro-life activities — Human dignity and human rights — Silence is concurrence and complicity — Continuing Holocaust — Deceptive euphemism

Prayers for Our Nation and the World 271

A Prayer for Guidance 271
A Prayer for Legislators and Judges 272
A Prayer for Courage, Faith and Hope 273
A Prayer To Secure Our God-Given Rights 274
A Prayer for a Reawakening of Moral Sensitivity 276
A Prayer To Understand Our Starving Brothers 278
A Prayer for Social Justice and Charity 279
A Prayer for the Common Good 280
A Prayer for a New Birth of Freedom Under God 282
A Prayer for the Right to Life 283
A Prayer To Safeguard Our Sacred Rights 284
A Prayer To Renew Our Society 286

International Relations

Address at the NCCW Painesville Deanery, Annual Diocesan Luncheon, on May 2, 1957.

It may seem a bit presumptuous for us to venture into the wide field of international relations—a field which challenges and seems to defy the best efforts of statesmen and social and political experts of the world, working through and apart from the United Nations. And yet, since the maintenance of peace in the world is of interest to all of us, we should at least know and appreciate certain fundamental principles which must serve as the basis for any plan for world peace.

We are not all in a position to know and understand the complex issues and problems which are currently a threat to world peace. We should, however, try to appreciate the elementary principles which must govern the efforts to attain world peace.

As Catholics, we should consider not only the social and juridical approach to peaceful relations, but also the religious approach to peace.

Social-religious approach

Peace is the harmonious living of human beings in a permanent national and international social and juridical order. Peace is the fruit of justice.

Twice in the past forty years, we were forced into devastating wars. We met the challenge with the full force of our ingenuity, resources and patriotism. Fired by the earnest desire to garner from our sacrifices nothing other than a just and lasting peace for ourselves and all the world, we won, at an incalculable price, a great martial victory.

Armed victory may remove some obstacles to peace, but it cannot make or insure a lasting peace. Unless we have the vision of a good and lasting peace, and the *will* to demand it, our bloody victories will be a hollow and even a tragic thing. We met the challenge of war. We continue to face and must meet the challenge of peace.

Peace demands a plan based on sane realism

Every society, every nation, has originated in a desire for peace and, hence, aims at attaining that peace. War was not caused by primitives or unlettered people. It was the result of *bad* education—a clash of ideologies. Some scholars, ignoring the innate rights of men, families and minority groups in their civil and religious life, created a system of monstrous philosophies which did not recognize the true nature and destiny of man, and the nature and function of the State. They confused and distorted the notion of the common good. They created the monster of absolute supremacy of the State with the consequent enslavement of human beings, subordinating their very life to the "good" of the State, which, too often, was determined by the caprice of a personal or party dictator. The gilded dreams of a new era heralded by these systems proved to be a hideous nightmare.

Effective negotiations for peace demand a good plan—a plan which states principles in terms of all the specific questions at issue; a plan which not only uses the same words, but also attaches the same meaning to the words. Restoration of peace demands sane realism regarding the nature and purpose of man. Unless there is a basic agreement on what man really is, there is no way out of the confusion and conflict which block the road to real peace.

Problem of man is basic

The problem of man is basic to all problems of peace. A sane and realistic concept of man's origin and destiny is the first principle, the starting point for any plan for peace. All discussions about peace must be focused on man.

In the Providence of God, man existed before the State. The human society extends beyond the boundaries of any country and continent. It is composed not of a collection of nations, but of a community of individuals bound by a single law of charity based on their common nature and origin and destiny, and by which they are bound to one another as members of the same human family.

Man is destined to live in civil society. He is a social creature, and needs the benefit of social society for his own preservation and development. Since it is practically impossible that all men, in such great diversity of places, of climates, of traditions and of habits, should form one sole civil society with common laws and common superiors, there is, by moral necessity, a division of the human family into nations.

The essential elements of the human family and of civilization transcend the particular bounds of geography, circumstances, race, language, political regime, the arts, etc. The cause of science and culture is not identified with national groupings, but freely crosses national frontiers for the benefit of the entire human family. The contributions of Pasteur, Galileo, Curie, Shakespeare, Sienkiewicz, Dostojevsky, Bell, etc., quite naturally become the patrimony of the entire human family.

By divine Providence, the earth is the "nursing mother" of all, and was created for the use of all human beings. This disposition and distribution of natural resources, in different geographical sections, calls for a social-economic interdependence of the human family across national lines. This interdependence is made more imperative by modern civilization and intercommunication.

The State is not a transcendental entity, having its own end, but, as a union of individuals who are not only social entities, but also personal beings, it has an end which includes the perfection and happiness of every individual. The State exists not for itself, but for man. Man is not a creature of the State, but rather, the State is a creature of man. The State must protect man and safeguard his inalienable rights, and in pursuing this objective it cannot ignore the needs of the entire human family. These are basic principles which must be agreed upon as a foundation for any peace movement.

The nation

The object and purpose of a nation—of government in law—is well illustrated in the American concept of government, which is founded on the premise that man has inalienable rights from God; the function of the State is to protect these rights.

Those who framed our Constitution were firm and explicit in the conviction that God and God-given rights must be recognized. They were firm and explicit in their conviction that religion and morality are the strong supports of the national well-being; that national morality cannot prevail in the absence of religious principles, and that the impartial encouragement of religious influence on its citizens is a proper and practical function of good government.

Patriotism

The "Fatherland" is the co-parent of the individual. Parents give physical life to the individual. The Fatherland, with its traditions, culture, language, customs, etc., gives intellectual life and development to the individual.

From the love of parents it is easy to pass to love of country. They are in the same category of obligations. St. Thomas Aquinas (II-IIae, q. 101, a. 1) explained this point in this way:

"Man is a debtor to others according to their excellence and diverse benefits received from them. Under both aspects God holds the highest place, because He is the most excellent and first principle of our being and of our government. The secondary principles of our being and of our government are our parents and our country, from whom and in which we are born. Therefore, after God, man is, above all, debtor to his parents and to his country. Hence, since it is the duty of religion to honor God, in a secondary manner it is the duty of *piety* to honor our parents and our country."

Patriotism is, therefore, a manifestation of that species of charity which is called *piety*. Catholic morality, which commands love of country, sanctifies and purifies it and defends it from the deviations to which it is at times exposed.

Patriotism and peace

Sound patriotism contributes to peace of nation and to international peace. Love of country and of nation, which is natural and strong, is, in itself, an impulse to virtue. It causes all citizens to desire their own nation to be distinguished among other nations, and this desire logically moves each one to cooperate for the glory of country with his virtue, with his labor, and with his sacrifices.

Sound patriotism follows the middle course between two extremes of *exaggerated nationalism* and of *false internationalism*. The former feeds on hatred for other nations, and desires to trample them underfoot. The latter denies the reality of country and, together with country, all the noblest ideals.

Sound patriotism does not ignore the fundamental law of Christian love between all human beings. It recognizes the existence of the human family. Sound patriotism is a love of nation, which is a love of *preference*, not of *exclusion*.

When kept within these bounds, patriotism is not only a virtue, but it is a source of national and international peace. Sound patriotism — which recognizes the origin, nature, function and destiny of man and of the nation — contributes to world peace.

The religious approach to peace

Our efforts in the modern secularistic world must be patterned on supernatural realities. There is in the world today a very dangerous trend, emanating from two distinct sources, which would keep separate the temporal and the spiritual orders. The secularists, who ignore the reality of God, insist on absolute separation of the two orders. Extreme pietists would substitute piety for competence in the temporal order.

The temporal and spiritual orders are indeed distinct, but certainly need not be separate. Human nature and divine nature are distinct realities in Christ, but united in His Person. His humanity did not suffer from the union, but was ineffably glorified and enriched. Nor was divinity diminished, for only by becoming man could Christ give us the supreme evidence of God's love for man by dying for us as a man.

In the spiritual order, the plane of the Church, all our actions are directed toward eternal values: toward God and the things of God, toward the goal of eternal life.

In the temporal order, the plane of the world, our actions are directed toward the goods of time. As citizens, we take part in the affairs of humanity in time. We work for values in the intellectual or moral order—in the work of civilization, culture, the sciences or arts, the political, economic and social exigencies of daily living. These are real values.

The basis for such work in both the spiritual and temporal order can be found in the doctrine of Christ's Mystical Body. This doctrine is expressed beautifully and repeatedly in St. Paul's epistles:

"I, therefore, exhort you to walk in a manner worthy of the calling with which you were called, with all humility and meekness, with patience, bearing with one another in love, careful to preserve the unity of the Spirit and the bond of *peace*."

"Rather are we to practice the truth in love, and so grow up in all things in him who is the head, Christ. For from him, the whole body (being closely joined and knit together through every joint of the system according to the functioning in due measure of each single part) derives its increase to the building up of itself in love" (Eph. 4).

Because we are all members of the same Mystical Body of Christ, we must be concerned about the welfare of each member of that Body. This is not the concern of priests only. It is true, as St. Paul tells us, that Christ "gave some men as apostles, and some as prophets, others again as evangelists, and others as pastors and teachers, in order to perfect the saints for a work of ministry, for building up the body of Christ until we all attain to the unity of faith—to the mature measure of the fullness of Christ."

However, while we do not all have the same duties and same authority within the Church, we are all members of the Church—Christ's Mystical Body. As Pius XII once said to some pilgrims in Rome: "You do not merely belong to the Church, you are the Church."

Because we are all members of the Mystical Body of Christ, we have a duty to all other members of the Body.

In helping others, we help Christ, and the records in heaven will so be kept and presented at judgment.

In pursuance of this doctrine of Christ's Mystical Body, the Catholic bishops of our country carry on the wide program of relief.

The Responsibility of Journalists to God and Society

Address at the Convention of the Religious Newswriters Association, on June 24, 1957.

Responding to your invitation, I shall express only my personal views, as a reader of your articles, as an individual clergyman of the Catholic Church, and as a native American who loves his country and is deeply concerned about its welfare. Though connected with one of the best diocesan newspapers in the country, I make no pretense at being a journalistic expert. For some years, I have dealt with the religious newswriters of our local secular papers. I venture to say that I have always been on cordial speaking terms with them, even though at times they are impatient because I do not always speak as much as, or at times when, they would want me to speak.

Need for reaffirmation of basic concepts

As religious newswriters, you must realize that basically the concept of religion implies a bond uniting man to God. It implies a recognition of God as the Creator and Ruler of the universe, as the Master of human life and destiny, and as the Judge of all mankind. It implies man's acknowledgement of his dependence upon God by acts of homage and by obedience to God's will. The supreme mission of the Church is to promote and preserve the most intimate union of man with God in time and for eternity, by promoting the sanctification and the salvation of man's immortal soul. The activity of the Church is not limited to religious services or to dogmatic pronouncements, but extends to every phase of human life and activity, insofar as it is related or has a bearing on the salvation of souls. The entire program of Church activity is coordinated and subordinated to the Church's mission of saving souls.

These basic concepts need reaffirmation because of a tendency in some religious sects to concentrate their efforts on the promotion of social adjustment and good fellowship between men, and, by default, to relegate the task of promoting good relations between man and God to secondary importance. When the pharisee lawyer asked which was the greatest commandment, our Lord answered, "You shall love the Lord your God.... This is the greatest and the first commandment, and the second is like it: You shall love your neighbor as yourself." The twin commandments of love are the inseparable sides of the coin of religion. The religion which neglects the greatest and the first commandment reduces itself to the stature of a fraternity with a program of vague humanism.

As religious newswriters, you must be alert to the concerted effort which is being made to exclude God from human living and thinking. A part of this effort stems from the shrewd and systematic campaign of atheistic communism against God and religion. This effort is wittingly aided by a secularist segment of our society. It is a small, but very articulate segment. It avoids theorizing about God's existence, but is determined to effect a practical exclusion of God and religion. The same effort is unwittingly aided by professional bigots, who focus their efforts against a particular religion, but in their total impact are carrying on a warfare against all religious influence.

One of the tactics of atheistic communism is to ridicule and discredit religion and religious leaders. They ignore the tremendous contributions of the religious, charitable and educational programs of the Church, but publicize the slightest divergencies between religious sects and leaders, far beyond the importance of the issues involved. They create the impression that religion is torn with strife; that it has a divisive influence upon the citizens of a country, and that dogmatic differences should be eliminated.

The success of such efforts in our national life is all too evident. In one instance, it has touched the very core of our national existence — the federal Constitution.

Interpreting the First Amendment

The First Amendment declares that "Congress shall make no law respecting an establishment of religion or prohibiting the free exercise thereof." For over a century, the simple and carefully phrased language of this clause was understood and interpreted in the sense intended and expressed by the framers of the Constitution. It simply restrained the federal government from establishing a single Church or religion enjoying formal, legal, official, monopolistic privilege through a union with the government. It placed no restriction upon the states, but allowed them full freedom in all matters of religion. It said nothing about schools or education, and contained no ban on equal aid to all religions; in fact, no ban on aid to one religion, except indirectly, if such aid be part of establishment. It said nothing about aid to religious establishments, which are quite different from an "establishment of religion."

In our own day, we have seen the simple and clear language of this amendment, without justification in constitutional history or in legal theory, distorted into a constitutional provision erecting a metaphorical wall of absolute separation between Church and State. It has been succinctly stated that:

"The militant secularists have scored three major victories in their campaign to keep religion within the four walls of the church building. Two of these victories were... the Everson and McCollum cases.... The third secularist victory is perhaps the greatest. Through clever propaganda, secularists have duped many people into thinking these decisions were warranted. They have shelved the actual wording of the First

Amendment, ignored its history, and substituted their favorite metaphor, 'the wall of separation between Church and State'" (Keefe, *American Separation of Church and State,* 9/11/51). This "wall of separation" has become a byword and is used not only to promote separation between Church and State, but even to promote hostility between the two.

The success of the clever propaganda of secularists is evident from the publicity given to, and the impact of the byword "wall of separation." There are many instances in which this byword is used to defeat the best interests of our country.

In October, 1951, the President of our country, acting, as he explained, "in the national interest" and with a view of "coordinating the effort to combat the Communist menace," nominated a diplomatic representative to the Vatican State, which, as he said, "is vigorously engaged in the struggle against Communism." He, and not the Vatican, initiated the idea. He did so in the "national interest." He did so with the knowledge that our country had consular representation in the Papal States from 1797 to 1848, and that with Senate approval, President Polk established a full diplomatic post in the Papal States which remained active from 1848 to 1867. He did so with the knowledge that close to fifty countries, many of them non-Catholic, maintained diplomatic representatives at the Vatican. He knew that France, Great Britain, India, China, Japan, Egypt, Iran, Finland, Syria and others were among those that maintained such representation at the Vatican. He did so with the knowledge that, for the best interests of our country, diplomatic relations were maintained even with the Soviets and Soviet-dominated countries. Despite the precedent in our history, despite the fact that he acted in the best interests of our country, the cry "wall of separation" was raised by an articulate minority, creating sufficient disturbance to nullify the President's plan.

That same cry is being raised again and again in what appears to be a determined effort to bar all religious influence in public education, and to liquidate the private school system. Charges are made that the private and religious school is un-American; that it is divisive, and that the public school system is the only true American school; that our American way of life can be safeguarded only by a monolithic educational structure controlled by the State.

Such statements betray crass ignorance of our national educational history, and of the democratic principles of our American way of life. A State-controlled one-school system is foreign to our national history, and contrary to democratic principles. Such a system is a prelude and fellow-traveler to the one political party, the one church and the one newspaper system, invariably found in totalitarian states. We can appreciate why dictators must have a State-controlled one-school system, but we fail to understand why any real American should confuse and identify educational uniformity with political unity. We are disturbed and alarmed by the intentions and actions of those who ignore the historical fact that the strength of our democracy lies in its ability to create political unity out of religious and cultural diversity, and that the "equal protection of law for all" implies the existence of diversity.

Even the extreme liberal, John Stuart Mill, warned us against educational monopoly in the words: "A general State education is a mere contrivance for molding people to be exactly like one another; and as the mold in which it casts them is that which pleases the predominant power in the government... in proportion as it is efficient and successful, it establishes a despotism over the mind leading by natural tendency to one over the body" *(On Liberty)*.

In his Farewell Address, Washington said that religion and morality were the indispensable supports of political prosperity, and that "whatever may be conceded to be the influence of refined education, reason and experience both forbid us to expect that national morality can prevail in exclusion of religious principles." Jefferson, who founded the University of Virginia, said that no education is complete without religion. The first Land-Grant College in this nation (Ohio University) traces its origin to a clause in the Northwest Territory Ordinance of 1878, which declared: "Religion, morality and knowledge being necessary to good government... schools and the means of education shall forever be encouraged."

When precisely did the teaching of morality and religion in schools become un-American? When did the teaching of subjects which were traditionally considered indispensable supports of political prosperity become a divisive element? How can religion, which teaches the essential principle of unification—that we are all children of God, all brothers, children of the same Father—be called divisive?

If a pluralistic school system is a threat to national unity, what is to be said about the pluralism of our political parties, of our newspapers, of our various religious sects, etc.? Must they all be liquidated and welded into one State party, State Newspaper, State Religion?

If the law and Commandments of God are banned because of the objections of a few, what about the laws of our land? I know that the criminals in our jails object to them. I know that many law-abiding citizens object to the laws which oblige us to pay a tax on our income. Since when do we abrogate laws that do not please all the people and introduce a note of unreasonable divisiveness?

Was there any evidence of divisiveness in the tens of thousands of graduates from religious schools who volunteered for services during the last war? Was there any difference in their loyalty and devotion to country noticed on the battlefields of the world? If there was, it was only that the graduate of the religious school was taught that service to country was not just a civil, but a moral and religious duty as well.

In further pursuance of their objectives, secularists would like to reduce all religions to a common denominator of beliefs and practices. They insist that if one faith is mentioned or represented, the others must also be mentioned or represented. They charge intolerance if one sect adheres firmly to its tenets....

Personally, I make a sincere effort to practice the virtue of charity towards all — believers and non-believers. I consider everyone, including the sinner, as my neighbor. But I am a Catholic because I am firmly convinced that it is the one and only true religion of God. I would like to share my faith with all, but I know faith is a grace of God, so I pray for all who are not of my faith.

Guiding public opinion in the path of truth and light

At this point, you may wonder whether I have stored a sufficient reserve of ammunition to fire a broadside at you. I promised not to flail or doublebarrel you with criticism. You are said to be in a breast-beating disposition. According to an ancient and currently valid spiritual practice, the breast-beating *mea culpa* follows an examination of conscience. In the light of my preceding remarks, I shall submit a few points for your examination of conscience.

As individuals and as religious newswriters, you have a responsibility to Almighty God, and some day He will judge you. You have the responsibility of promoting the knowledge of God, love for and obedience to Him among your readers. As journalists, you have the social responsibility of presenting the real news of the day objectively, without bias or prejudice, without distortion, in its true perspective, without overemphasizing the sensational, the bizzare, the ridiculous, and without featuring the unwholesome traits of odd publicity-seekers. You have the responsibility of not only presenting a true picture of the life of the day, but you help to make the life of the day by your influence upon public opinion. You have the responsibility of informing and guiding public opinion in the path of truth and light.

Your first obligation, as a religious newswriter, is to have a well-grounded knowledge of your subject. Journalistic experience and tricks of snappy reporting are no substitute for knowledge. You must inform and instruct, and not just entertain your readers. The simple reporting of schedules of religious services and of social events does not make you a religious newswriter any more than reporting the line-up for the day's game would make you a sportswriter. Knowing your subject, you must select events and statements which have substance and value, and present them accurately, completely, with appropriate background information and with some commentary.

With these points in mind, how would you answer the following questions:

Have you been a religious newswriter or an anti-religious newswriter?

Have you featured the irresponsible statements of professional baiters, when they used such terms against some form of religious belief or practice as "brainwashing," "circus—rock and roll tactics," "wall of separation," etc.?

Have you given a four-column headline to the petty criticism made to a ¾ empty church against an evangelist who had been drawing crowds of 15 to 19,000 every day for almost a month?

Have your articles featured the unwarranted charges made by secularists against the honest efforts of religious organizations and groups?

Have you ever tried to present the tremendous contributions of the religious, charitable and educational programs of religion to a particular community?

Have you given the impression to your readers that the occasional carping criticism of individuals reflects a constant strife and dissension among religious groups?

May I reassure you that I appreciate the obstacles under which you are forced to work.

You are subject to the tyranny of deadlines which force you to turn in incomplete work to impatient editors.

You are subject to the domination of the owners who control the papers, and your copy must, at times, be alert to their sensitivities and sympathies.

You are subject to the influence of your own personal beliefs which have a way of filtering through and affecting your choice and presentation of news.

You are subject to the demands of the readers, which tempts you to resort to slick-trick snappy reporting, and to cultivate a neutral and shallow type of journalism.

You are subject to the criticism of religious organizations and committees, which are jealous of any publicity given to others.

But with all these obstacles, your desires to improve the standards of religious journalism is a tribute to your professional honesty and integrity. You realize well that in journalism, as in other fields of endeavor, complacency is stagnancy, and self-satisfaction is deterioration. I offer my sincere congratulations to you. It is my fervent hope and prayer that you will persevere in your breast-beating attitude and that your improvement will redound to the glory of God and to the religious, moral and spiritual rebirth of the people of our nation.

God – the Source of Human Rights and Liberty

Address at the 76th Meeting Supreme Council Knights of Columbus States Dinner, on August 19, 1958.

The noble ideals which gave your organization its being and its wonderful growth are *charity, unity, fraternity* and *patriotism*. This evening, I direct your attention to and submit for your consideration some basic concepts relative to your ideal of *patriotism*.

St. Thomas tells us that it is a duty of religion to honor God, the first principle of our being, and a duty of piety to honor our parents and our country, from whom and in which we are born (*Sum. Theol.* II-II, q. 101, al). Parents, cooperating with God, give us our physical life, and our country—with its traditions, customs, language and culture—provides intellectual life and development. In this respect, our country is a "co-parent," and the same duty of piety which obliges us to love our parents also obliges us to love our country.

Man – a social creature

In the Providence of God, man is a social creature, destined to live not in isolation, but in a society. The human society is a community of individuals, bound by a single law of charity, based on man's common nature, origin and destiny. Since it is practically impossible for all men, living in such a great diversity of places, climates, traditions and habits to form a single, worldwide society, there exists a division of the human family into nations or States.

Man existed before the State. The State does not exist for itself, but for man, and is, in reality, a creature of man. It exists for the sake of protecting man, safeguarding his rights, and promoting his perfection and happiness. Although God did not create the State directly, He willed it, inasmuch as He placed in men a social impulse which induces them, in all times and places, to establish a State.

The State is not an arbitrary or artificial institution because it derives its authority from God. Christ told the Pharisees: "Render to Caesar the things that are Caesar's" (Mt. 22:21), and He told Pilate, "You would have no power at all over me were it not given you from above" (Jn. 19:11). St. Peter wrote: "Be subject, therefore, to every human creature for God's sake" (1 Pt. 2:13), and St. Paul said: "Let every soul be subject to higher powers; for there is no power but from God,... Wherefore be subject of necessity... for conscience' sake..." (Rom. 13:1-7). The fundamental fact of human existence is that God, the Creator and Ruler of the universe, has sovereign rights over individuals, families and nations. The cornerstone of all society is respect for legitimate authority. All must acknowledge the supreme rights of God, acknowledge their first allegiance to Him, and rulers must acknowledge that they hold their stewardship from God, and that, without God, there is no foundation for the observance of any law, and no safeguard for any human right.

A true patriot

Patriotism, or love of country, is a duty of piety—an impulse to virtue. It causes all citizens to desire their own nation to be distinguished above all others, and to cooperate with labor and sacrifice for the glory of their country. Sound patriotism follows the middle course between the extremes of exaggerated nationalism and false internationalism. The former feeds on the hatred of other nations, and desires to trample them underfoot. The latter denies the reality of country. Sound patriotism does not ignore the sovereign rights of God, nor the fundamental law of Christian love between all human beings. It recognizes the existence of the human family. It is a love of preference, not of exclusion. Within these bounds, patriotism is not only a virtue, but a source of national and international peace. Sound patriotism, which recognizes the supreme authority of God, and the nature, origin, function and destiny of man, contributes to peace, order and happiness.

Conversely, love of country, based on a denial or a practical exclusion of God and His supreme authority, is not true patriotism, but an aberration which has repeatedly led to national and international havoc. The man who denies or ignores God's existence and authority regards the human individual as a creature of the State, who has no rights except those accorded to him by the State. He denies individual freedom and regards the individual as a mere cog in a social machine designed and operated by an elite of social engineers. He considers man as a functional worker, on the level with a bee, who must be provided with the security of a hive at the price of his person and his freedom. The atheist and secularist who denies or ignores the existence of God denies or ignores the vital and basic philosophy of our national Constitution. Consequently, he cannot truly love his country; he cannot be a true patriot, and, in fact, he cannot, in genuine sincerity and conviction, pledge allegiance to the American flag. A true patriot must desire and work for national morale. There can be no national morale without national morality, and the Father of our country solemnly assured us that national morality cannot exist without religion.

This point was brought out with incisive clearness by His Holiness, Pope Pius XII, in his encyclical letter, *Meminisse Juvat*, of July 14, 1958: "But if we examine with thoughtful minds the causes of so many dangers, present and future, we can easily see that the decisions, forces and institutions of men are inevitably destined to fall short wherever the authority of God...is neglected, or is not given its just place or even is suppressed.... It is harmful and imprudent to come into conflict with the Christian religion, whose eternal duration is guaranteed by God, and proven by history. One should reflect that a state without religion cannot have moral rectitude or order. The formation of minds to justice, charity and obedience to just laws depends on it; it condemns and outlaws vice; it stimulates citizens to virtue, indeed controlling and regulating their public and private life."

The history of our country is the history of God-believing, God-loving and God-fearing men. Columbus, Vespucci and all the discoverers of the Pacific and of Mexico were Catholic. The Grand Canyon, Colorado and New Mexico were discovered by the Franciscan Marco da Nizza a hundred and thirty years before the landing of the Pilgrims. Pere Marquette explored the Mississippi. Father Kino drew the first map of California, while his confrere, Father Claudio, christened St. Joseph's Lake in Michigan. The Franciscan Serra was the apostle of California. Fathers Augustine and White were the first to compile grammars in the Indian language.

God — source of inalienable rights

The Continental Congress proclaimed July 21, 1775 as a day of public prayer and penance so that virtue and religion might flourish throughout the land. The Declaration of Independence acknowledges God as the Creator, Protector, Source of all inalienable rights, and supreme Judge of the world. The Constitutions of 48 states acknowledge God as the source of human rights and liberty. Each President of our country, in his inaugural address, professed his faith in God. In our national hymns, we proclaim God as our

Father, Author of liberty and as our King, and profess, "In God is our trust." We invoke God's name in pledging allegiance to the flag. "In God we trust" is stamped on our coins, and our one dollar bill depicts the ever-watchful "Eye of God" over the words *"Annuit Coeptis"* — meaning that God has favored our undertakings. Our President declared three years ago that, without God, there can be no form of American government or American way of life, and that the first and fundamental expression of Americanism is the acknowledgement of the Supreme Being.

The framers of our Constitution were firm and explicit in their conviction that God is our Creator and Source of our inalienable rights, which the State must protect. They were equally firm in the conviction that religion and morality are strong supports of our national well-being; that national morality cannot prevail in the absence of religious training and education, and that the impartial encouragement of religious influence on its citizens is a proper and practical function of good government.

In view of such a glorious history, it is most disturbing to note the progress being made by a very small, but very articulate segment of our society which is determined to effect a practical exclusion of God and religion from the life of our nation. This poses as a super-righteous defender of freedom.

Academic freedom

They protest against any criticism of what they would teach in classrooms with the cry:

"academic freedom." But academic freedom, just as any other freedom, has attendant and inseparable limitations. The teacher is free to present the truth, but he cannot use his position to pass off personal views, opinions or errors as truth. He must label his "wares," and he must show due consideration for the laws of his country, the policies of the educational institution, and the wishes of the parents of his students.

Freedom of speech

In recent years, we have seen a great deal of offensive rot peddled from book and magazine stands. Some of this, after liberal doses of detergents, and dressed in fancy trappings, is transferred to the screen as "adult fare," but the ad writers try to sell their denatured wares on the notoriety of the original. The minute any decent group of citizens protests against such demoralizing and degenerating literature or movies, a cry of "Freedom of Speech" is raised. They condemn such "censorship" and protest that a minority are trying to impose their concept of morality on a majority. In reality, freedom of speech and expression has limitations, and it must be curtailed at all times in the interest of truth, decency and national security. Moreover, consumer criticism and consumer protest is, in reality, an exercise of the freedom of speech and expression.

Freedom for religion

There are even some groups which point a finger of accusation at Catholics and the Catholic

Church, and raise the cry "Freedom of Religion," implying thereby that the Church will somehow force all to be Catholic. Though this cry scarcely warrants comment, Pope Leo XIII, in his encyclical *Immortale Dei*, clearly states: "In fact, the Church is wont to take earnest heed that no one shall be forced to embrace the Catholic Faith against his will, for as St. Augustine wisely reminds us, 'Man cannot believe otherwise than of his own free will.'" Yes, we desire and pray for the conversion of all, but the Church never has, and never will, force anyone to embrace the Catholic Faith against his will.

It appears that this small but articulate segment in our country is determined to pursue a course which is foreign to the intentions and expressed convictions of our Founding Fathers, and to the glorious traditions of our country. They seem determined to dissipate the spiritual and moral capital amassed through the years; to demoralize and degenerate the living habits of our generation, and to reduce and shut off the influence of religion and morality, which is so necessary for our national welfare. They fail to realize that no nation can achieve greatness on material values alone. It needs spiritual and intellectual values. Material values are consumed and spent. Without spiritual values, a nation will deteriorate into anarchy and barbarism. They seem determined to produce religious and moral starvation and, thereby, effect freedom *from* instead of freedom *for* religion!

I chose to speak to you on the subject of patriotism — one of the four ideals of your organization—for more than one reason. I had hoped to evince that your religious-rooted patriotism is true American patriotism; that your interest in and contribution to the Catholic school system is of incalculable value to your Church and to your country; that by your efforts to promote the knowledge and practice of religion and morality, you are rendering a service of true Catholic Action to your bishops and to your Church, and a patriotic service to your country; that by your interest and your aid to Catholic Youth Organizations, to Newman Clubs, etc., you are promoting national morality which is essential for national morale.

In brief, I have tried to point out that, by your example and by your deeds, you bear with dignity and worthiness, the name of a Catholic Organization—the title, *Knights of Columbus*. May God's most abundant blessings attend all your noble efforts as faithfully as do my prayerful best wishes.

A Return to Complete Truth

Address at the Dinner Meeting of the Ohio Prosecutors Association, on March 4, 1960.

About twenty years ago, in completing the requirements for a Doctorate in Canon Law, I wrote a book on the rights of the defendant. My attraction to the poor defendant was abruptly reversed by my appointment to the office of Promoter of Justice in the Diocese of Cleveland — an office equivalent to that of a Prosecuting Attorney in civil law.

As lawyers, you practice the art of applying legal rules to facts. Your proficiency in this field merited the confidence of the voters, who entrusted you with the office of Prosecuting Attorney, with the sacred charge of safeguarding public order and the common good. If your record of dispatching cases approaches that of the Prosecutor of Cuyahoga County, you more than justify the voters' confidence, and you deserve the highest praise and congratulations for your devotion to the duties of your office.

Legal learning and philosophy

In view of your rich experience in the practical field of your profession, it would be a presumptuous waste of precious time to speak on any practical phase of your work. Accordingly, with full appreciation of the limited time you have for study, I venture to focus your attention on a wider field of your profession, namely, that of Jurisprudence, with special emphasis on the true Philosophy of Law.

Cicero tells us that "legal learning [should be] drawn deep from philosophy and held dearly" (*De Legibus*, Bk. 1, n. 5), and Wigmore adds that "every institute and principle of law has a philosophy" (*The Law of Torts*, Preface). Justice Cardozo wrote: "Implicit in every decision where the question is so to speak at large is a philosophy of the origin and aim of law, a philosophy which, however veiled, is in truth the final arbiter" (*The Growth of Law*, II, p. 25). On the subject of "The Bar and Legal Education" (23, *American Bar Association Journal*, 926), Dr. R. M. Hutchins of the University of Chicago said: "At some stage of his education, and I should hope in his study of metaphysics and the philosophy of nature, the student should learn that in order for a thing to change, it must first be, and that the causes of its being are not the same as the causes of its changing.... Hence, he will be able to withstand the skeptic and the sophist; he will know that everything is not a matter of opinion; that the truth is not what suits our convenience or prejudices; that good is not a matter of taste. He will know that man is not the measure of all things, but that man is measured by the truth, which is the conformity of his intellect to reality, and by goodness, which is the conformity of his will to objective moral standards."

Americans take pride in being a practical people, but their emphasis on the practical, at times, neglects the theoretical aspects essential for a thorough understanding of a profession. In the legal profession, this trend reflects itself in a tendency to treat law as a mere collection — to use Coleridge's phrase — "of marbles in a bag that touch without adhering, and overlook law as a system."

A thorough grasp of certain philosophical principles

A lawyer must master the art of applying legal rules to facts, but such mastery is unachievable without a thorough grasp of certain philosophical principles that are necessary to understand, clarify and apply the laws. This is particularly true in the realm of criminal law, which deals with human conduct.

What, precisely, is philosophy? It is the knowledge of things through their ultimate causes; it asks the last how, why, of what and whence. Philosophy of law is a science which investigates the essential nature, the origin or ultimate source, and the development or history of law.

The science of law tells us what the law *says*. The history of law tells us whence and how the law came. Philosophy of law tells us what the law — in abstract — is, and what the law — in the concrete — should be. The function of philosophy of law is to consider law in the abstract and to define it; to determine the relation between law and all else in the world; to investigate the law's ultimate sources or universal basis; and to deduce from the ultimate purpose of law the necessary rules which govern all human activity in which law is enacted, interpreted and applied.

One who knows what the law says and whence it came is a jurist. One who knows current law and applies it is a counsellor. One who knows not only singular facts and technical procedures, but also the universal principles of reason — applicable to the case at hand — is a legal philosopher, or a master of jurisprudence. Jurisprudence is a coalescence of philosophy, history, and the special art of applying the law to facts.

Various schools of philosophy

It has been said that there are at least fifty-seven varieties of legal theory and political philosophy. Certainly, on the question of the origin, or ultimate source of law, there are at least eighteen schools of philosophy. These schools propose various theories, such as the social contract, institutional, rationalist, liberalist, historical, evolutionary, individualist-utilitarian, positivist, coercive power, dialectical-materialist, social-utilitarian, collectivist, national-socialist, idealist, sociological, subjectivist, and the natural law.

These various schools can be reduced to two general categories, viz., the traditional school of Natural Law, which, until the severance of Christian unity in Europe, was practically the only school of thought. The idea of the natural law was expressed by Hebrew prophets, Greek philosophers, Roman jurists, and was developed in its fine points in the Christian Era. English lawyers invoked this law and American lawyers wove its doctrines into the texture of the Declaration of Independence. With the rupture of Christian unity in the 16th century, there appeared by way of reaction against the Church a materialistic philosophy, which was subsequently applied in the field of jurisprudence, and gave birth to the School of Juridical Positivism.

Natural law jurisprudence

The traditional philosophy of American Law is the Natural Law Jurisprudence. Our Founding Fathers were quite clear, in their private statements and in the Declaration of Independence, in acknowledging the "Law of nature and nature's God" as the source of human rights, and in proclaiming that human rights are not derived from human power or laws, but from God: "We hold these truths to be self-evident, that all men are created equal, that they are endowed by their Creator with certain unalienable rights, that among these are life, liberty and the pursuit of happiness."

Positive law jurisprudence

Though the traditional philosophy of American Law has been the Natural Law School of Jurisprudence, there have been manifestations of the Positive Law School of Jurisprudence, such as the School of Realism, with Robinson, Llewellyn, Corwin, Frank and Beutel; the School of

Economic Determinism with Adams, Bear and Bohlen; and the School of Sociological Jurisprudence with Pound, Cardozo and others.

Holmes was the forerunner and inspiration for the Positivistic spirit in American Jurisprudence. His influence is still current in our schools and courts of law. He tried to dismiss Natural Law as a product of wishful thinking. He insisted that physical force is the essence of law: "the will of the sovereign is law because he has power to compel obedience or punish disobedience and for no other reason" ("The Path of Law," *Coll. Legal Papers*, p. 169). He insisted that right is not a postulate of a pre-existing framework within which a law must operate, but is actually a product of the law: I think that the sacredness of human life is a purely municipal ideal of no validity outside the jurisdiction.... I see no reason for attributing to man a significance different in kind from that which belongs to a baboon or a grain of sand" (Holmes-Pollock, *Letters*, Vol. II. pp. 13, 36, 252). He insisted on divorcing all considerations of morality from the law, insisting, for example, that the violation of a contract entailed no more than liability for damages. He explained: "But such a mode of looking at the matter stinks in the nostrils of those who think it advantageous to get as much ethics into the law as they can" (*Path of Law*, p. 172). He maintained that preference determined moral good and moral evil; that, in the final analysis, approving or disapproving Lesbianism has the same objective value as liking or not liking sugar in coffee (H-P *Letters*, I. p. 105). He rejected the idea of absolute rights, and the possibility of absolute truth, and once said that "truth was the majority vote of that nation that could lick all the others" ("Natural Law," *C.L. Papers*, p. 310). He considered that the sanctity of human life was much overrated, and said: "I shall think socialism begins to be entitled to serious treatment when and not before it takes life in hand and prevents the continuance of the unfit" (*Book Notices*, p. 181; *C.L. Papers*, "Ideals and Doubts," p. 306).

Holmes' greatest contribution to jurisprudence was that he drew logical inferences from his theories, and these inferences form the sound basis for absolute totalitarianism, rather than for our form of government.

The currency of his influence is evident from a statement made in the past decade by the late Chief Justice Vinson: "Nothing is more certain in modern society than the principle that there are no absolutes, that a name, a phrase, a standard has meaning only when associated with the considerations which give birth to the nomenclature. To those who would paralyze our government in the face of impending threat by encasing it in a semantic straight jacket, we must reply that all concepts are relative." If Holmes and Vinson were correct, then the principles of our Declaration of Independence on the rights of man lack solid foundation.

A return to natural law jurisprudence

In 1951, Herbert Hoover, speaking of our nation, said: "Our greatest danger is not from invasion from foreign armies. Our dangers are that we may commit suicide from within by complaisance with evil. Or by public tolerance of scandalous behavior. Or by cynical acceptance of dishonor."

I would like to add that a very real danger of national suicide comes from those who have discarded the traditional philosophy of American law, i.e., Natural Law Jurisprudence, and have adopted and try to apply alien philosophies of law, which not only contradict, but sweep aside the very foundation of our national form of government and our American way of life.

The legal philosophy of Holmes, and of those who consciously or unconsciously adopt and apply his views, is a philosophy which can be used to justify all the atrocities perpetrated by the absolute totalitarian forms of government which have created and maintain world disorder, and which ignore the dignity of man and the sanctity of his rights and of his life.

It is for this reason that I make a fervent plea to you in behalf of Jurisprudence and the true philosophy of law. By reason of your profession, and by reason of your love for our beloved country, you should acquire not only a thorough knowledge of what the law says and means, but also a thorough knowledge of what the law is in relation to its ultimate sources, and what it should be. My plea is for a return to complete truth; to the traditional American philosophy of law—the philosophy which acknowledges the "Law of nature and nature's God," and which, alone, can safeguard the inalienable rights we derive from our Creator. The Natural Law philosophy is woven into the texture of the Declaration of Independence, and, if we are to survive, it must be the guiding philosophy in our legislative assemblies and in our judicial processes.

The Church in Defense of Man's Dignity

Address at the Diocesan Council of Catholic Youth, 9th Annual Convention, on May 1, 1960.

It is a pleasant duty to present this award for apostolic leadership to the individuals selected by the Diocesan Council of Catholic Youth for such recognition. It is a comforting thought that the youth of the diocese observe and compliment those who let the light of their good works shine before men, and acknowledge them as models of participation in the apostolic mission of the Church.

Christ established the Church and determined the eternal salvation of the individual as the principal and ultimate objective of its apostolic mission. This mission is premised on the reality that life in time upon earth is a prologue to life in eternity which, alone, is true life, because it knows not death. The reality of man's eternal destiny was evinced by Christ's own life, passion, death and resurrection.

Affirming the individual

Though the chief preoccupation of the Church is man's eternal destiny, it has, since its founding, faced the necessity of being concerned with man's temporal life — the prologue of eternity. Time and again, it rises to the defense of the human individual — defending his sublime dignity and rights against forces which try to minimize, disintegrate and even annihilate the human person.

The necessity of defending the individual is urgent even today. The world is being consumed with a raging fever for discovery. The tremendous resources of God's creation are being uncovered. Awesome distances are spanned with supersonic speed. The barriers of the skies are being passed, and plans for the conquest of planetary regions and the invasion of farthermost stellar spaces are being drafted.

While the glories of creation are being unfolded, the glory, the sublime dignity and spiritual destiny of the most noble creature — made to the image and likeness of God — is being neglected or sacrificed. The created universe is insignificant in value, compared to the value of man's soul, which God cherishes the most.

Christ, the Son of God, became man for the sake of man, shedding His own blood for man's ransom. Man is the adopted child of God, and by the gift of grace shares God's own life and nature. God lavishes upon man the most precious gift of gifts — that incredible freedom by virtue of which he is to serve God, but with which, to his own detriment, he can also venture to defy and even to deny God Himself! The Church and religion exist for the sake of man. Man is the all-important thing in the world, and the Church has been constant in affirming, defending and guarding man's dignity, rights and spiritual destiny.

Since all men are made to the image and likeness of God, all are equal. To defend this equality, the Church took issue with the Roman Empire, which kept two thirds of its population in slavery. It took issue with all theories of super-racism, apartheidism and segregationism, by word and example, conferring high honors and offices upon peoples of every race and color within its fold.

The Church has ever defended the dignity of womanhood. Roman law regarded woman as a chattel — a piece of property — owned by her husband and completely subject to his whims and fancies. The Church, pointing to the example of the Mother of God, insisted on the dignity and rights of the wife, the mother and the daughter. Even today, it resists the influences which tend to ignore the noble qualities of a woman's mind and heart, and to overemphasize her physical attractiveness, thereby obscuring her individuality.

Since the year 1500, efforts to downgrade, devaluate, disintegrate and even annihilate man have come from all sources. Luther and Calvin denied man all capacity for good, claiming that original sin destroyed all such capacity, and that salvation came entirely from grace, with no cooperation or good deeds from man. Others minimized the part played by the human will in a meritorious act.

Some regarded man as a mere worker or producer — as a creature of the State, as a member of a class, as a victim of heredity and of circumstances, as the victim of class conflict and endless social change. One science after another examines man and explains him in terms of psychology, zoology, biology, chemistry, electricity and as an atom in an amorphous mass.

The right to liberty and to life

In the wake of such devaluation and disintegration of man, there has followed a challenge and even violation of man's right to liberty and even life itself.

An entire continent lies crushed under the heel of the most massive and absolute cruelty. Man is denied religious, civil and domestic liberty. Even in the free world the basic rights of man are challenged. The right to live is denied under the cry of "population explosion." The right of the unborn is challenged by so-called therapeutic or economic and socially motivated abortion. The right of the deformed, crippled, aged and ailing is challenged by euthanasia — and even the fancy name of "mercy killing" does not render it aught else but murder. The right of the weak, the criminal and the insane to bodily integrity is challenged by the proposal of sterilization of the "unfit."

Even such quasi-religious movements as Quietism and Romanticism — which proclaim the autonomy of passions, futility of law, the vanity of theological thought — reduce man to a helpless victim of impulse and sentiment. Quietism tries to abolish the human person, and have him absorbed in a mysterious and vague mystical union. This form of withdrawal from social and true spiritual life is a type of self-annihilation which seems to appeal to some of today's youth.

Modernism regards man as a spark in a flaming mass; as an organism conditioned by the laws of chemistry, physics and biology; as a creature subject to physiological reflexes; as a walking theorem, having a consciousness which is no more than a thread of events—a variable resultant of the multiple facts and complexes of life.

The Church's defense in word and in deed

While this conflict against man continues unabated, the lone voice of the Church rises in protest and in defense of man's dignity, rights and spiritual destiny. The Church proclaims that every person is the child of God, and the king in the universe. She defends the man in the Siberian prison and work camps; the displaced man in refugee camps; the dark, yellow and red-skinned man, as well as the white man; the man in Africa, China, Russia, as well as the man in America. She defends the poor and the rich man; the learned and the illiterate; the free and the slave; the healthy and the sick; the virtuous, as well as the criminal man. She proclaims all men to be potentially adopted children of God; redeemed by Christ's precious blood, living in time for eternity, and having a spiritual destiny to which all things must be subordinated and coordinated.

The Church proclaims the eternal truth that everything in this world exists for the sake of man. The state does not exist for its own sake; art does not exist for art's sake. Social reforms do not exist for their own sake. All scientific progress, all productivity, all economic development do not exist for their own sake, but for the sake of man. Man—his life, his liberty, his rights—may not be ignored or sacrificed; neither may his opportunity to pursue his spiritual destiny be impeded or inhibited.

The Church proclaims these truths in defense of the human individual not only in words, but in deeds. It maintains infant homes, orphanages, homes for wayward girls and boys, hospitals and homes for the sick and ailing, homes for the aged and dying. In addition, it provides loving care, social and spiritual services to every home and public institution where human misery can be found. It also maintains a vast system of schools to teach man about his own dignity and his destiny. The Church proclaims and defends the rights of man in word and in deed.

The Church's vast program in defense of man is carried on with the zealous support and generous cooperation of the laity. Lay persons devote their time and talents to the various phases of the Church's apostolic mission. Their contribution is vitally important. Their example, especially to the young, is priceless in value.

That is why it is such a genuine and great pleasure to hail and to congratulate today's recipients of this special award and to encourage them and others to continue the shining example of their apostolic leadership in their respective fields. It is also a pleasure to assure them that today's award is but a token and a pledge of the far greater reward in eternity which awaits all who love God and love their fellow men.

The Substance of Your Profession — Justice and Love

Address to the St. Thomas More Society of Philadelphia, on September 17, 1961.

"Blessed are they who walk in the law of the Lord. Blessed are they that keep his precepts" (Ps. 118).

Continuing the seven-century-old tradition of the "Red Mass," we have, under the sponsorship of the St. Thomas More Society, assembled this morning to implore the inspiration and guidance of the Holy Spirit for all members of the bench and bar in the current and coming terms of court.

Traditionally, judges and doctors of law attended this Mass in the distinctive robes of office. The color of their robes matched the deep liturgical red of the vestments of the Mass of the Holy Spirit — symbolic of the flame of God's love.

The welcome presence of judges, lawyers and government officials, so pleasing to God and to us, reflects nobility of character and a sense of deep responsibility to God — the source of all wisdom, authority and law. Your public act of worship is a humble acknowledgment of human frailty and dependence upon God. It gives glory to God, edification to the people you serve, and stirs our hearts anew with the vision of the city of God and brotherly love.

Religion—the parent of law

By happy coincidence, today is also Constitution Day. It is most fitting that we who live in the "Cradle of Independence," and in the shadow of the hall where this great document was framed, should prayerfully commemorate the juridical act which safeguards the dignity and freedom bestowed upon man by his Creator.

On an occasion such as this, it is well to recall the role of religion in a democracy. The prime function of democracy is to protect the inalienable rights derived from the natural law. This law, which derives from God, is immutable. It antecedes all human enactments and contrivances. It is the only foundation upon which the structure of our democracy can rest secure. Religion, which relates man to God, exerts a socially cohesive influence. Without religion, democracy is meaningless and will degenerate into anarchy and terminate in despotism. Tragic proof of this is evident in the atheistic and secular governments which are the cause of so much mischief and evil in the world today.

Religion is the basis of culture and the parent of law. The oldest known civilizations acknowledged the fact that law is the child of religion.

In the most ancient Sumerian civilization, the temple was the court of law, and disputes were settled before the throne of their god. The black diorite column in the Louvre Museum of Paris has a relief of King Hammurabi receiving the code, the masterpiece of ancient jurisprudence, from Shamash, the divine patron of justice. Even when the court was separated from the temple, religion was still the support of law. In the Roman civilization, a crime was punished as a disturbance of the order of heaven.

The Mosaic code of laws—with the Ten Commandments—was the foundation of the revealed religion of Israel. It embraced ritualistic, moral, social and economic laws. It was the law of the community, directing the whole life of the people. Israel's kings were its judges, exercising judgment upon the people.

The Canon Law of the Church is called "the nurse and tutor of common law" of the Anglo-Saxon tradition. The moving spirit behind the Magna Carta was Cardinal Stephen Langton, Archbishop of Canterbury.

The formative days of American jurisprudence are reminiscent of the days of the Magna Carta. The Founding Fathers clearly and forcibly brought out the religious foundations of law. Jefferson said: "The God who gave us life, gave us liberty at the same time." Hamilton wrote: "The sacred rights of mankind are not to be rummaged for among old parchments or musty records. They are written, as with a sunbeam, in the whole volume of human nature, by the hand of Divinity itself." From the earliest days of our national history, the essential importance of God, religion and morality were acknowledged in theory and in practice. High officials in every branch of our government, and our official motto, "In God We Trust," proclaim that religion is the sovereign authority in the United States. Thus the Founding Fathers saw it, and with God's help it will continue to be.

The jurist's vision

The jurist worthy of the name, though not a theologian, must be capable of rising to the vision of the highest transcendental Reality — God, from whose will is derived the order of the visible universe. The jurist, to appreciate and apply the mutable laws governing social relations, must appreciate the immutable laws of the eternal Judge, upon which all laws are based. The jurist must be capable of moving between the finite and the Infinite, between the Divine and the human.

In dealing with Constitutional problems the jurist must appreciate the fact that the Constitution is the juridical act of the people, not that of their Congress; that the highest aim of the Constitution is to protect the freedom and the dignity of man by imposing severe and enforceable limitations upon the freedom of the State.

The Constitution provides a plan for government to last for centuries. It is the expression of the will of the people, and, as such, is subject to change by the people. The continuity of the Constitution must be assured. Such assurance demands flexibility in interpretation. Elected branches of government must exercise discretion so that society may, by its own democratic decisions, adapt itself to circumstances which are vastly different from those which existed in the isolated agricultural communities of Constitutional days.

Unless there be such flexibility in interpretation and adaptation to new circumstances, the Constitution may serve to trample upon the very essential rights which it was designed to preserve. The gravest offenses against justice happened not so much in opposition to the laws, but through the very laws. This was true centuries ago, when Cicero wrote: "Summum jus, summa iniuria" *(De Officiis,* 1.10.33): highest law—highest injustice. It has been true in our own days, when the laws in some states infringed upon the essential rights of the human personality, even though such rights were solemnly proclaimed and guaranteed by the Constitution of the same states.

There is a segment of people in our country who are inclined to attach a dogmatic value to the Constitution. They raise the cry of "unconstitutional" to honest efforts to interpret flexibly and adapt the provisions of the Constitution to promote equal justice under the law. They betray ignorance of the fundamental difference between the immutability of God's laws and the changeability of human laws.

Our Constitutional democracy can survive only if the force of law and governmental power be interpreted in terms of religion—the highest moral insights regarding man's true nature in relation to God. Law and government trace their source to God Himself.

The great responsibilities entrusted to you by your fellow citizens, as makers, interpreters and administrators of the law, carry a divine sanction. In performing your duties, in pursuing and promoting justice for all, you will merit God's blessings.

May God grant you the enlightenment promised to those who walk in His law and His love. May He give you the courage to pursue the substance of your profession, which is justice, and also the essence of your lives, which is love — love of God and of your neighbor.

The Nation of Immigrants

Address at a banquet of the American Committee on Italian Migration, on January 7, 1962.

Twice before it was my pleasure to address in public gathering the Cleveland Chapter of the American Committee on Italian Migration. Today, it is my pleasant privilege to address the Philadelphia Chapter as it and ACIM celebrate their tenth anniversary of charitable action. Though my acquaintance with the individual members of your Chapter is not as intimate as it was with the members of the Cleveland Chapter, I am well acquainted with the ideals and achievements of your organization, and I am properly at home in your presence.

Working with the various Diocesan Resettlement Offices and within the existing federal laws, ACIM has helped 125,000 Italian emigrants — over the annual quotas assigned to Italy — to find homes and jobs in the United States. ACIM accomplished this result, not by pressure tactics, but by an intelligent educational program which stirred the consciences of the people of the United States and our legislators to the inadequacy and unfairness of our immigration policies. This achievement, praiseworthy in itself, produced collateral benefits for peoples of other nations. In addition to the Italian emigrant, some 300,000 refugees, migrants and relatives from other countries benefited by the initiative and imaginative efforts of ACIM.

The Philadelphia Chapter of ACIM was established almost with the birth of the National Committee ten years ago—under the spiritual direction of Monsignor Pasto and the chairmanship of Americo Cortese. This able leadership has continued under your President, Mr. Frank Carano. Men and women of outstanding character have held office and still do in the Chapter of Philadelphia.

Your work merits the highest praise. As leaders in a charitable work, you represent the thousands of citizens of Italian ancestry in our community. You have helped over 500 Italian emigrants, about 100 families, to find new and happy roots in the United States. You have ever concerned yourselves with settling and assisting emigrant Italian families. Our Holy Father, Pope John XXIII, recently spoke of this basic problem:

"Those who are responsible for emigrants and refugees will not forget that the family remains an untouchable haven for the migrant, where he restores his energies, finds himself again, and receives the strength for a new effort.

"According to general opinion, it also represents his best chance for integration into the human community. Therefore, it is our ardent hope that religious and civil institutions will be able to favor the regrouping of family units, even at the price of heavy sacrifice, providing for them suitable lodgings and the means of educating their children by the opening of day nurseries and Catholic schools" (Pope John XXIII to Emigration Council, October 20, 1961).

The basic human right to migrate

Though I could well sing the praises of your achievements, I deem it more profitable to your work to speak about the principles and ideals which have motivated your efforts—the basic human right to migrate.

In the Providence of God, all men, created to His image and likeness, are bound by a solidarity which transcends national, political, geographic and racial barriers. All men are members of the same human family—all were created by God; all were redeemed by Him; all were created for Him. All have a right to the riches of this earth, and all have the responsibility of making these riches available to all members of the entire human family.

The phenomenon of migration is a historical fact rooted in the natural law. The physical world is subject to a law which stirs and mixes the elements of life without destroying them. Organisms born in a certain spot are transported and scattered from place to place. Seeds migrate on the swirling winds. The currents of oceans and rivers sweep plants and flowers from one shore to another. Birds and animals migrate as a means of self-preservation. In like manner, man migrates to escape want or political, religious or racial persecution, and to secure bread and peace. His Holiness, Pope John XXIII, speaking to the Eleventh Conference of the Food and Agricultural Organization of the United Nations, said:

"Today's world is aspiring to two great ends: peace and bread. Peace has its source in man's faithfulness to the demands of the Our Father; this produces, in turn, like a natural fruit, the well-being, which we know to be the gift of divine Providence. 'Give us this day our daily bread...' and one may say that those who are giving bread to hundreds of undernourished human beings are working to give peace to humanity—peace that will always be in danger as long as economic imbalance between nations continues to exist" (Pope John XXIII to Eleventh Conference of FAO, Vatican, November 23, 1961).

Migration is a natural, inalienable human right which the State—or rather the States—are obliged to recognize, respect and protect. However, this fact does not prevent, but emphasizes the necessity of human action regulating and guiding emigration, so that it may fulfill more fully its natural object which is "the more advantageous distribution of humanity on the surface of the earth" (Pius XII, on the 50th Anniversary of *Rerum Novarum*).

In implementing this natural right of migration, every government has the duty to protect its natural interests, and the right to set up regulatory laws of entry. But natural interests should not be exaggerated, much less used as a screen for discrimination on the basis of racial or religious prejudices. At the present time, approximately 50,000 visas available annually to the people of Great Britain, Ireland and Germany are not used. On the other hand, countries with small quotas have a staggering number of petitions registered under the four preferential quotas established in our immigration laws. At the present time 140,000 of these petitions are for Italy, and this ever-increasing backlog can be resolved by the allocation of approximately 50,000 yearly visas unused by the northern countries.

Italy provides a classical example of this critical problem of migration. It has approximately 115,800 square miles, only about half of which is arable. Italy is one-fifth the size of Alaska (586,400); less than one-half the size of Texas (267,339); about two-thirds the size of California (158,692); less than one-half the size of Montana (147,138); less than the size of New Mexico (121,666); and only a little larger than Arizona (113,909).

Italy has a population of about 50,000,000 trying to eke out a living in sixty-five thousand arable square miles. Alaska, Montana, and New Mexico are each larger in area than Italy and each has a population of approximately a million people.

Migration brings social peace

The people of Italy do not ask for charity, but for an opportunity to work for themselves in a dignified manner. They seek the peace of heart which comes to an individual who has escaped want, or to a father who has found a better tomorrow for his children. Migration will help to bring peace to such persons, and social peace to a nation that suffers from overpopulation and unemployment. Every able-bodied man should have the chance to obtain the employment he urgently needs to provide daily bread for himself and his family.

A new evaluation of our present immigration laws, and a more just allocation of quotas would relieve somewhat the problems of modern Italy, whose heritage and culture you fondly cherish and we gratefully share, and whose emigrant sons—"tired and poor and yearning to breathe free"—attracted by the bright torch of the Statue of Liberty, have contributed their talents to making the United States the greatest country in the world!

Emigration opens the door to a threefold blessing—the immigrant finds a new home, a new country, new opportunities; the country of origin is relieved of a burden; the receiving country is enriched with new spiritual and physical forces.

Your work in the interest of justice must be adorned with the warm glow of charity. While pursuing justice, you must never lose sight of the charity which helps others and rewards yourselves. In his Christmas message of 1961, Pope John XXIII said:

"Men are meant to understand, to help and to complete one another by brotherly cooperation, by patiently overcoming differences and by sharing the goods of the earth fairly—*justitia duce, caritate comite*—"justice leading, accompanied by charity.'

"The Sacred Scriptures speak with clarity about love of neighbor for the love of God. The prophet Isaiah says:

"'Ease the insupportable burden, set free the overdriven; away with every yoke that galls! Share your bread with the hungry, give the poor and the vagrant a welcome to your house; meet the naked, clothe him; from your own flesh and blood turn not away, and the Lord will give you rest continually, and fill your soul with comfort' (58:6-7)."

With complete trust and confidence in God, let us carry out His command to share our bread with the hungry; our land with the oppressed; our job opportunities with the needy; our homes with the uprooted and tempest-tossed peoples of the world. Let us be true to the traditions of our beloved country—the nation of immigrants, the home of exiles.

This evening, in this tenth anniversary year, I congratulate the National Organization of ACIM and, in particular, the Philadelphia Chapter for your very effective charitable and educational program. You are implementing the fundamental human right to migrate. You have heeded the law of charity and followed the command of Christ, who on the flight into Egypt was Himself an emigrant. I pray that you will see Christ in the guise of the immigrant, and that one day you will hear His words: "Come, blessed of my Father, for I was a stranger and you took me in."

Immigration — a Matter of Natural and Positive Law

Address at the Third Annual Greater Philadelphia Conference on American Immigration Policy, Citizenship, and Refugee Matters, on December 15, 1964.

Over the years, the question of immigration has been a matter of special concern to me. For that reason, I welcomed your kind invitation to address the Third Annual Greater Philadelphia Conference on American Immigration Policy, Citizenship and Refugee Matters.

In the Providence of God, all men created to His image and likeness are bound by a solidarity which transcends national, political, geographic and racial barriers. All men are members of the same human family. All have a right to the riches of this earth and the responsibility of making these riches available to all members of the huge human family.

The phenomenon of migration is an historical fact and a natural law. The physical world is subject to a law which stirs and mixes the elements of life without destroying them. Organisms born in a certain spot are transported and scattered from place to place. Seeds migrate on the swirling winds. Fish, birds, and animals migrate as a means of self-preservation. In like manner, man migrates to escape want or political, religious, or racial persecution.

Migration is a natural, inalienable human right which the State is obliged to recognize, respect and protect. However, this fact does not prevent, but emphasizes the necessity of human action regulating and guiding emigration, so that it may fulfill its natural object which Pope Pius XII described as "the more advantageous distribution of humanity on the surface of the earth" (50th Anniversary of *Rerum Novarum*).

A passage from the profound social document of our late beloved Pope John, *Pacem in Terris*, summarizes these truths: "...Among the rights of the human person there must be included the one by which a man may enter a political community where he hopes he can more fittingly provide a future for himself and his dependents. Wherefore, as far as the common good rightly understood permits, it is the duty of the State to accept such immigrants and to help integrate them into itself as new members."

Political, social and economic considerations are factors in the determination of a nation's immigration policy. However, a nation's moral sense, its values and traditions, its attitude toward the realization of the common good, the very way in which it looks upon itself, these also are inseparable from the way it treats strangers desiring to dwell within its confines.

Part of our national interest

No one seriously proposes that unrestricted immigration be restored by the United States. But even so, is it not true that we experience a warm nostalgia and sense of pride when we hear the words inscribed on the Statue of Liberty:

> Give me your tired, your poor,
> Your huddled masses yearning to breathe free,
> The wretched refuse of your teeming shores.
> Send them, the homeless, tempest tossed, to me.
> I lift my lamp beside the golden door.

Maintain the national interest, yes; but is not the preservation of these sentiments and ideals a deep and integral part of our national interest?

The national and international implications of immigration policies have grown increasingly more complex and sensitive. Someone has aptly described our time as the Era of the Dispossessed, a time of upheaval and mass shifting of people. Populations are rapidly increasing. Automation is changing the structure of industry and business, while the labor force grows but cannot adapt quickly to automation, since the labor force is people, not machines. Any attempt to enact a new set of immigration laws in the changing context of the present day world would be fraught with problems, and rightly should be subject to critical analysis.

As a matter of fact, many persons have strongly criticized the current immigration law.

Robert F. Kennedy said that the present law is "a standing affront to millions of our citizens and our friends abroad." Presidents Eisenhower, Kennedy, and Johnson have all said that new immigration legislation is a necessity. Countless articles, speeches, and group proposals have given insistent expression to that judgment; yet despite this concerted effort, the 1952 law remains.

This has been a source of discouragement and frustration to many. But it only serves to demonstrate that laws are enacted or changed only where there is a demand for action. The call has not been long, loud, or clear enough to prompt the people in large numbers to recognize that a change in the immigration policy is for the national interest. Voters are not easily aroused to consider issues which do not touch upon their immediate concerns.

Let the law reflect the heart of America

It is not necessary to review for this gathering the history of the immigration policy of America, nor to speak about the statistics of population projections, shifts in the labor force, or the other factors which condition the standard of living. These are matters for the experts to study and debate. But the recommendations resulting from these studies should reflect the confident optimism of the American people. The immigration policy of a nation mirrors its image of itself. Is it our wish to advertize America to the world as a nation whose dynamism is grinding to a halt and whose genius to absorb and become enriched by diverse elements is beginning to ebb?

Many call for a change in our immigration policy to improve America's image abroad. This is indeed a valid concern. We do live in a community of nations, and we wish to leave to future generations an America which enjoys good relations with other peoples. This is surely a part of our national interest. But even more important than how other people see us is how we see ourselves. We must be true to ourselves as a nation, to the traditions and principles which have given growth to America. Fear, overcautiousness, national selfishness should not form the basis of any American policy.

A revision or modernization of the immigration policy, to be realistic, needs restrictions and controls, quantitatively first of all, to determine an annual quota consistent with the needs and capacities of America; but also qualitatively, to guard against the entry of subversives and criminals, and to encourage the coming of the especially skilled and the talented. An honest appraisal of the national interest—an honest appraisal, not nearsighted, gloomy, or complacent—should be the basis of the law; but let the law also be enlivened by the spirit of justice and compassion which reflects the heart of America.

You are all familiar with the evolution and present provisions of the National Origins Quota system. Prescinding from the motives of those who enacted this system into law, it must be stated that the practical consequences of it are a matter of deep concern. May I just say that, for very personal reasons, I am happy that it was not in effect at the turn of the century. For perhaps if it were, two young people from Eastern Europe might not have been able to come to this country, settle here, marry and raise eight children to enjoy America's blessings and, in some measure, I trust, bring credit to her good name.

Immigration—a matter of law

Immigration is a matter of law—of natural law and positive law. Just as the Constitution gives expression to the natural rights of man, so also should the immigration law be in accord with the inalienable human right of migration. It is within the framework of law that the phenomenon of immigration has to take place. If the law is not flexible enough to allow the problems of immigration to be faced on the human level in a just and compassionate way, then the law should be modified. Your organizations—by your experience, by the information at your disposal, and by the generosity of your members giving of their time and energy—are in a position to carry on a constructive program of education to create a favorable climate for immigration and of persuasion to elicit the public support necessary to prompt the debate and modification of the present immigration policy.

Immigration — a matter of people

But immigration is not only a matter of law; it is far more poignantly a matter of people. The most direct problems that are faced are neither political nor technical. Rather, they are questions which the human and social actuality pose. As Pope John said elsewhere in *Pacem in Terris:*

"The sentiment of universal fatherhood which the Lord has placed in our heart makes us feel profound sadness in considering the phenomenon of political refugees, a phenomenon which has assumed large proportions and which always hides numberless acute sufferings."

We may say the same regarding all persons who have been uprooted, who have to be resettled and readjusted to a new way of life. This pastoral solicitude accounts for the efforts of the Catholic Church to form and maintain national parishes to meet the needs of immigrant peoples. These parishes enable these people to preserve and strengthen their religious life and customs, and to enjoy the great consolation of worshipping and confessing in their mother tongue. They have provided in the course of time for the transition of the children of these people into the more general American way of life which has thereby been greatly enriched.

The physical, psychological and spiritual well-being of immigrants, whether voluntary or refugees, is the real field for your work. Experience has shown that even so human a thing as having a familiar meal may be a matter of great importance to a recent arrival. Far more important are his family ties, his manner of worship, his loneliness and heartaches of separation, and his feelings of inferiority.

You have lent yourselves to assisting in these difficulties, confronting those who for various reasons must leave their homeland to seek spiritual and economic betterment in America. I commend you for your generosity and effective efforts, and end by reminding you of the words of Isaiah the prophet:

"Share your bread with the hungry, and bring the needy and the harborless into your house. When you shall see one naked, cover him, and despise not your own flesh. Then shall your light break forth as the morning..., and your justice shall go before your face and the glory of the Lord shall gather you up" (58:7, 8).

May almighty God bless and prosper your work.

Neither Apathy, nor Indifference, nor Complacency, but Action

Address at the Christian Weekend Retreat, on January 24, 1965.

The imitation of Christ in our lives has been the theme of this retreat. The central question has been: How would our Lord act if He were in our place? Our prayer has been to find the answer to that question, and to acquire the strength and purpose to act accordingly.

Christian action

Toward this end, then, it is proper that in this last meditation we devote our reflection to the problems of prejudice and poverty. Abstract expressions of belief to many seem remote and unrelated to actual situations. The truth which is at the root of this feeling is that words without deeds may sometimes be more blameworthy than silence, as St. John has said: "Little children, let us love in deed and in truth and not merely talk about it" (1 Jn. 3:18).

But action unanchored in perennial principles of justice and charity can wreak even more havoc. The devotees of Nazism and Communism are activists of the first order, but their activities have scarred not only their victims, but also themselves, for by acting out pernicious principles, they engrained them more deeply into their own consciousness. That this is no idle concern is readily apparent when one listens to spokesmen calling for conflict and the acquisition of power as the only possible course to compel change. Such statements always imply and frequently make explicit an attack upon charity as an effective instrument in the affairs of men. What our Lord described as the first and greatest commandment is belittled and pictured as inevitably producing vain self-satisfaction in some, and obsequious subservience in others.

In the face of injustice and suffering of any sort, the Christian has a personal mandate to act; but his action must be clearly stamped and easily recognized as Christian action. Otherwise, his efforts will be self-defeating and untrue to his deepest self and the vocation he received in Baptism. All this in no way militates against action in concert with others; for as Popes John and Paul and other religious leaders have insistently pointed out, there are many basic principles shared by Christians, Jews, and others alike which prompt rather than prevent common action by all men of good will. But sometimes the desire of being involved and of approaching the modern mentality can lead to a rejection of the forms proper to Christian life and even to rejection of the very dignity that must give meaning and strength to all eagerness for action. And thus, the true efficacy of the Christian apostolate can be vainly sacrificed to a useless imitation.

The dissolution of prejudice and the establishment of racial rapport calls for many interlocking efforts: social, economic, and educational. Hostility is not neutralized nor is good will generated by benign complacency. But the cornerstone of all eforts has to be a full-hearted determination, on the part of all, to get along with one another. We are not dealing merely with a socio-economic problem. It is far more importantly a matter of personal relations involving the hearts and minds of human beings. But attitudes and actions flow from the inner vision that men have of one another. In this regard, I would like to quote from a statement of the Catholic Bishops of the United States:

"The heart of the race question is moral and religious. It concerns the rights of men and our attitude toward our fellow man. If our attitude is governed by the great Christian law of love of neighbor and respect for his rights, then we can work out harmoniously the techniques for making legal, educational, and social adjustments. But if our hearts are poisoned by hatred, or even indifference toward the welfare and rights of our fellow men, then our nation faces a grave internal crisis" (1958).

The hour of charity

The focal point of all efforts is charity, the law of love of neighbor. Our concern is that charity should assume its rightful position, that it should indeed become operative where it is so deeply needed. It is not easy to subject this sublime virtue to a theoretical analysis. Our Lord Himself, the greatest of all teachers, taught it not so much by words, but by living it. Those around Him recognized it; they heard it in His voice; they saw it in His eyes; they felt it in the warmth of His presence. So difficult is it to capture charity in words, that the Father, wishing to reveal this law to man, could do so only through *the* Word, who is His own divine Son.

The charity of our Lord toward His eternal Father was not difficult, but to love us He immersed Himself in the harsh realities of humanity; He became man and experienced the failings and ingratitude of the sons of Adam. It is easy for us to love Christ, the perfect man, in whom there is no unpleasantness, no ugliness. But, like Christ, our love of neighbor means putting ourselves in one another's place, trying to feel what each feels amid the harsh realities of the daily ebb and flow of life. This is the Christian's challenge now in what might be called the hour of charity.

Good laws and their just application, education and governmental programs, community action, yes, all these things are necessary, but however much one seeks for answers, there remains the law of charity as *the* Christian formula for social relations. For charity explains all things. Charity inspires all things. Charity makes all things possible. Charity renews all things. Charity "sustains, believes, hopes, endures to the last" (1 Cor. 13:7). Charity is strong to heal, is sensitive to the human person, knows what it is about, and is not afraid to act. Through it the ordinary and seemingly insignificant events of daily life can be transformed and become occasions of courtesies and kindnesses which, when multiplied a million times daily, most surely bring the healing balm of the divine presence to bear on the disorders and injustices around us.

True, Christian social doctrine does not allow for apathy, indifference, or complacency; its proclamation must result in concerned action, but action whose driving force is love, not power, or fear, or resentment. If it is objected that such teaching is irrelevant and unrealistic, history says otherwise. All the armies ever assembled, all the navies ever built, all the parliaments which have ever convened have not affected the course of man's destiny as much as the life of a single man who summarized His whole teaching with the injunction that "greater love than this no man has, that a man should lay down his life for his friends."

Poverty and prejudice

Prejudice is difficult to get in proper perspective; it is engulfed in so much that is false and irrational. But certainly one characteristic of it is the despicable attitude of always thinking the worst of a whole group of people and of quickly grasping at isolated incidents to justify sweeping accusations. Racial prejudice has the special feature of failing to distinguish between race and social conditions as the source of much that is found disagreeable in the actions and attitudes of others. Violence and disregard for the law and the rights of others cannot be justified, much less condoned, no matter who does it; but poverty and frustration do leave their mark on families and individuals as well.

Those of you who are over forty years old can remember those days we now refer to as "the Great Depression." You remember the closing of factories and plants, the "runs" on the banks, the long bread lines, the apple sellers on the street corners, the scrip money, the hunger marchers, the "Brother Can You Spare a Dime" theme which expressed our national mood.

There are other things which you perhaps also remember, things which are closer to the heart. Maybe you remember the hopeless look in your father's eyes as he returned from another day's fruitless search for work, the increased appearance of brisket and corn meal on the family menu, the slow and unrelenting sinking into debt, and finally the acceptance of poverty as the way things are going to be.

But, as you let your mind go back to those days, you may not be aware, be really aware, that for thousands of your neighbors "the Great Depression" has never ended. Not far from your home there are hundreds of families who still struggle for the bare necessities of life, still hope for a better place to live, still search for jobs which do not seem to exist. These people are caught in the vicious cycle of poverty and prejudice—living in overcrowded, dilapidated homes, rearing children in an atmosphere of hopelessness.

For these unfortunate people, however, there is a great difference. For they are surrounded by the affluent society, an economy that is booming, the highest standard of living on earth. They see the finest schools in the world being built in every community but their own. True, it is easy to say, "Others have done it; let them do the same." But that is to succumb to the un-Christian attitude of "do unto others as has been done unto you," rather than to follow the teachings of our Lord, who said "Do unto others as you would have them do unto you."

It has always been the firm conviction and constant teaching of Christianity that the family is the basic unit of society. The sanctity of the home is a sacred heritage which we would see shared by all families; but regretfully the words of Pope Pius XII spoken several decades ago still apply to many sections of our city today:

"Truly the mind shudders when we recall how often the present economic scheme and particularly the shameful housing conditions create obstacles to the family bond and the intimacy of family life" (On the Construction of the Social Order).

Yes, our Lord did say, "The poor you have always with you." But, how tragic a mistake it would be to understand those words as implying acceptance rather than presenting a challenge. A retreat, I suppose, is not a time to discuss the techniques of social change, but it is a time to foster personal concern, a concern that should begin from within. Examine your conscience. It may be that the feelings you have for other people are the very same feelings your parents or grandparents faced when they "got off the boat."

As a climax of this unique retreat may I offer for your voluntary acceptance the following pledge:

"Recognizing my personal and social responsibilities as a follower of Christ, and fully aware of His clear teachings, I pledge myself solemnly to banish racial prejudice from my own heart and home, and from every sphere of life over which I exert influence. I promise that by earnest prayer and positive action I will endeavor to bring about more quickly the day when all men will be universally accepted as equal members of our human society, as children of one Father in heaven, with a common destiny of union with Him for all eternity."

May almighty God grant His choicest blessings upon you and your loved ones.

No Cultural Uniformity, but Political Unity

Address at the 28th Biennial Convention of the Grand Lodge of Pennsylvania of the Order of the Sons of Italy in America, on June 26, 1965.

The pleasure of accepting your compliments affords me a welcome opportunity to compliment you and similar ethnic and national groups for your continued vigorous, fraternal, charitable and welfare programs in the community, and also for being important columns, supporting the social structure of our American society.

The very existence of the Order of the Sons of Italy and similar national organizations is a surprise and a disappointment to some sociologists. Your survival, fifty years after the period of mass immigration to the United States, is a contradiction to sociological theories, which were proposed with an air of prophecy and infallibility for more than a century. These theories were accepted by some as unquestionable doctrine. They served as a basis for certain sociological movements. The goal of these movements was cultural uniformity. However, in their final impact, they were responsible for a great deal of divisiveness. The mischief they caused is responsible for some of the current problems which beset our American community.

Certain sociological movements

More than one hundred years ago, some budding sociologists advanced the theory of total passive assimilation of the various cultures of the people in our country. They proposed a process of intensive purification and purgation of the dross of foreignism and the consequent emergence of the 100% pure and unadulterated American and American culture.

In the course of the past century, these theories were translated into action by a wide variety of groups—too numerous to mention on this occasion. History records the activities of these groups and the mischief they caused. May I presume upon your patience by citing a few illustrations.

In this very city of brotherly love, a group labeled as "Nativists" carried on a vigorous and at times violent campaign to rid the community of what they considered foreignism. Their prime targets were the foreign-language immigrants: their culture, traditions, and even their religion. It is a fact that in a blighted era of our great city's history, Catholic churches were set on fire. These "Nativists" were forerunners of a variety of similar groups, some of which were, and still are, generally described by the word WASP — which is an abbreviation of the words: White, Anglo-Saxon, and Protestant.

The same sociological theory spawned the organization we know as the *Ku Klux Klan*. The

Klan set out to "protect" the American society from the Negro. While the Klan was preoccupied with the emancipated Negroes in the South, in the North a group was formed under the title A.P.A. — American Protective Association — which directed its efforts principally against the Catholic Church.

In the post Civil War period, some of the A.P.A. groups conceived the idea of using the public schools to grind down and out the traces of Catholicism. The public schools at that time were Protestant orientated. The reading of the Protestant Bible, the recitation of prayers in Protestant formulas, and even the teaching of Protestant doctrine was not only permitted, but compulsory. Traces of these practices were ruled out in recent years by the Supreme Court.

When the protests of the Catholics availed nothing, the bishops at the Baltimore Council enacted legislation calling for the establishment of parochial schools. The A.P.A. groups countered by introducing into the various state constitutions legislation prohibiting the diversion of tax funds toward private and parochial school education. These prohibitions were adopted by a number of states in the last half and the last quarter of the 19th century. As recently as forty years ago, an attempt was made to compel all parents to send their children to public schools. However, in the Oregon case the civil courts reaffirmed the right of parents to choose the type of education they wanted for their children. Within the past decade, California was the scene of a bitter battle to eliminate economic sanctions against parochial schools by compelling them to pay taxes. Fortunately, the traditional sense of justice of the American people prevailed.

Since 1870, the Congress has been beset by the problem of federal aid to education. Time and again efforts were made to enact legislation which would discriminate against an American child in American private and parochial schools. But Congress found means to provide educational aid, e.g., to children in impacted and impoverished areas and to veterans. These acts demonstrated that government can aid the education of children and adults, without depriving them of the freedom to pursue their education in a particular school, and at the same time without giving aid to a particular religious sect.

Theory of total assimilation

The same sociological theories of the 100% American are largely responsible for the present discriminating quota system of immigration. To quote from the Encyclopedia Britannica (Vol. 22, p. 844), the 1924 quota system was adopted to correct the complaints "that in the previous two decades the greater part of the immigrants came from southern and eastern Europe and was made up of persons who were not by tradition and inheritance of the same type as most of the previous immigrants." We are still trying to rid our country of the discrimination contained in the 1924 quota system of immigration.

The sociological theory of total assimilation was given increased currency by the naive and sentimental play about American immigrants written by Israel Zangwill in 1908. The play, entitled "The Melting Pot," captured the imagination of theater-goers. America was represented as a great melting pot into which immigrants of all origins, classes, and kinds were dumped unceremoniously, and from which they were supposed to emerge after intensive purification as 100% pure and unadulterated Americans.

We would hope that this unrealistic "Melting Pot" theory be discarded in our enlightened age. It has been proved wrong. Yet, its exponents persist in their efforts to apply it to daily life. We witnessed such efforts recently in our struggle to have the bus legislation enacted. Some of the most articulate opponents of the bill advanced arguments which sounded like a "broken record" from the 19th century. The comparison is not original. It appeared less than two years ago in an editorial in the Protestant magazine, *Christianity and Crisis*. The editors, including such eminent Protestant leaders as Rheinhold Niebuhr and MacAfee Brown, pleaded for a fresh approach to the problem of aid to education.

They complained that the "professional Protestant" approaches the problem with arguments which sound like a broken record from the 19th century. It is most encouraging that such eminent leaders and many Protestant groups approach the problem with the question: "What is good for American society and for the American child?" instead of the trite terms of the "wall of separation." There should not, and must not, be any wall preventing legislators from promoting the welfare of the total American society and of *all* American children.

The same sociological theory was applied at times in more subtle methods. Immigrants and their children were advised that they could not advance socially, economically, or politically, unless they shed their foreign-sounding names, their cultural heritage, and even their religion. They were urged to join certain societies with the promise of advancement.

Principle of integration of cultures

The social philosophy of the Catholic Church, which embraces all the peoples and races of the world, rejected the assimilation theory in principle and in practice. In our own city, Bishop Neumann took pride in mastering a number of languages. He invited the first groups of Italian immigrants to his own chapel and instructed them in their mother language. He established the first national parish in this country for Italians. Throughout the United States, bishops established foreign language parishes and schools. They encouraged immigrants to preserve their cultural heritage. They encouraged the preservation and propagation of the rich diversity of racial and ethnic cultures and gifts for the sake of giving the individuals pride of ancestral roots, and for the sake of enriching the culture of our

American society. They acted with the conviction that a man who denies an alien origin and who ignores his ancestral heritage is a man without roots; a man who does not respect his own past admits inferiority, and will not gain the respect of others. The social philosophy of the Church accepts the principle of integration of cultures, rather than assimilation by a melting process.

We might ask what the correct American view of the various cultures which came to our country with immigrants is? The Great Seal of the United States portrays a soaring eagle. Above it is a strand of ribbon carrying the words: *E pluribus Unum*—literally saying—"Out of many—One" and popularly translated: "Political unity of the widest diversity." This motto has been the boast of our country. It had opened its doors wide to the hungry, the tired, and poor of the world. It offered warm shelter to the refugees, and to the persecuted. It did so without any federal law or policy to hammer, melt or mold its people into one type or form. In fact, it has boasted of being a pluralistic society—a society of plural cultures, religions, schools, charitable institutions, political parties, and national and ethnic groups. I submit that the motto on the Great Seal of our Federal Government, *E pluribus unum,* and the guaranteed freedoms for individuals and groups, set the principle for a truly pluralistic society: a society in which the rich variety of cultural and ethnic groups enjoy the right of free assembly —the right to exist, and the right to resist all and any attempts at assimilation, at amalgamation, at being dumped into a melting pot.

It is my firm conviction that the sociological principle of integration is the only truly American principle of social evolution. It is the only principle that is supported by the reality of history. It is the principle that has been tried and tested under fire. In the Second World War, in Korea, and in Vietnam, American soldiers, of different ethnic backgrounds, of different color and race, educated in different schools—public, private, and parochial—and of different political persuasions, moved abreast in the face of enemy fire. Italo-Americans fought in Italy; German-Americans fought in Germany. Catholic Americans fought in Catholic countries and Protestant Americans fought in Protestant countries. They fought as true and loyal Americans. They risked their lives, shed their blood, and some made the supreme sacrifice of laying down their lives for the America they cherished and loved. What further evidence, what further proof can be demanded that our country is and should be a pluralistic society?

Despite such conclusive proof, there are some vocal elements in our country that still demand uniformity rather than political unity. They clamor for a one-school system, claiming that non-public schools are divisive. They resent the fact that various groups are engaged in conducting private charitable institutions and programs. They would have the State or community have exclusive control of such institutions and programs. They would have the State ignore the principle of subsidiarity, and take over that which the citizens are able and willing to do for themselves and for their neighbors. They would have the State monopolize all the areas of human life. In reality, they would have the State become totalitarian, and eventually move toward a one-school system, one political party, and a one press system. Such monopoly, such totalitarianism, such State absolutism is certainly not American.

Today, as you honor me, I compliment and congratulate you. I salute you, the officers and members of the Grand Lodge of Pennsylvania of the Order of the Sons of Italy in America, for what you represent, for what you are, and for the good things you do. Your Order, together with other similar organizations, forms the sparkling components of the brilliant vari-colored mosaic that is our beloved country. Together with others, you preserve the religious and cultural heritage of your ancestry and thereby enrich and strengthen the cultural structure of America. Together with others you constitute the plurality out of which is formed the strong unity of the country we love and cherish so dearly — the United States of America.

May God bless and keep you and prosper all your good works for the benefit of each other, the community, and the nation.

The Duty of Government — To Promote and Protect the Rights of Men

Sermon for the 7th Annual Observance of Sts. Cyril and Methodius Heritage Day, on July 13, 1969.

"Regardless of the changes which followed one another in the vicissitudes of time throughout the centuries, that vein of gold brought to you by Cyril and Methodius, with the tradition of faith and of spiritual values, has never become exhausted. Truly that vein of gold... did not become impoverished, but has grown greater, translating itself more and more in your literary, artistic and scientific creativity" (Pope Paul VI, June 20, 1969, to pilgrims from Czechoslovakia).

Apostles of many Slavic peoples

In a letter (February 2, 1969) commemorating the anniversary of St. Cyril's death, our Holy Father noted that many flourishing nations, with proper pride, proclaim the holy heralds of the Gospel, Sts. Cyril and Methodius, as their apostles. Through their ministry and that of their disciples the light of the Gospel was carried to the Moravians, Slovaks, Slovenes, Bohemians,

Poles and Croats, Serbs, Macedonians, Bulgarians, Ukrainians, Russians and White Ruthenians. Our Holy Father noted that Sts. Cyril and Methodius must be considered as gentle and stable patterns of Christian charity and brotherly communion which unite all of the peoples who trace their religious heritage to them.

We assemble today to pay tribute and honor to Sts. Cyril and Methodius through fervent prayer. We pray with the conviction that these saints certainly desire and are able, with greater efficacy and power than they had on earth, to bring light, strength and victory to the various trials to which the peoples whom they evangelized are subjected.

A service of prayer for a just and lasting peace

While our motives and objectives are primarily religious, they do have corollary values to our country and to the world. In July of 1959 the 86th Congress passed a resolution requesting and authorizing the President to issue each year, "until such time as freedom and independence shall be achieved for all the captive nations of the world," a proclamation designating the third week of July as *captive nations week*. In that resolution Congress adverted to "the enslavement of a substantial part of the world's population by Communist imperialism"; that "the imperialistic policies of Communist Russia have led through direct and indirect aggression to the substantial subjugation and material dependence of Poland,

Hungary, Lithuania, Ukraine, Czechoslavakia... and others." Congress declared: "It is vital to the national security of the United States that the desire for liberty and independence on the part of these conquered nations should be steadfastly kept alive.

While our prime purpose this morning is to pray and to seek the intercession of the great apostles, Sts. Cyril and Methodius, this very religious act of prayer serves as a deterrent to war and an encouragement for a just and lasting peace, and is a vital service to the security of our own nation.

Religious freedom

This morning we can profitably reflect upon the principles of religious freedom. It is an essential duty of government to promote and to protect the inviolable rights of man. Principal among these is the right to religious freedom. This right has its foundation in the very dignity of the human person, as the dignity is known through the revealed word of God, and by reason itself.

God, the Creator of the universe, directs and governs it and all the ways of human community by His law. Man was made by God to participate in this law. Because God endowed man with reason and free will and the capacity to bear personal responsibility, man is impelled by nature and bound by a moral obligation to seek truth. He must especially seek religious truth so that he may know his origin, his nature, his destiny, and thus form for himself the right and the true judgments of conscience. Man's quest for religious truth, in accord with his social nature, is an obligation and an inviolable right which cannot be abrogated or impeded by any human authority — by any government.

It follows that government does wrong when it imposes upon people by force, fear or any other means the profession or the repudiation of any religion. Religious freedom is so essential and so basic that its repression renders insecure every other human freedom, every other human right.

The Second Vatican Council made it clear that the use of force to repress religion is a violation of the will of God and of the sacred rights of a human person. This same principle is found in Article 18 of the Universal Declaration of Human Rights, which reads:

"Everyone has the right to freedom of thought, conscience and religion,... and freedom either alone or in community with others and in public or private to manifest his religion or belief in teaching, practicing, worship and observance."

We pray for victims of militant atheism

Today, through the intercession of Sts. Cyril and Methodius, we beg God to restore the blessings of freedom to all who suffer unjustly repression, persecution and enslavement. We pray, in particular, for all those whose Christian heritage came through the two great apostles whom we honor today. We pray for all people who are targets of militant atheism. We pray for those who are subject to a campaign of intimidation, terror and violence designed to eliminate religious belief and religious practices. We pray for those Churches that are deprived in part, or in whole, of the use of the means of social communication instruments in proclaiming the Gospel. We pray for all Churches that are the targets and victims of domination or suppression. We pray for all people, especially the young, who are subjected to a relentless barrage of the intensive indoctrination of atheism.

After fifty years of relentless effort, atheistic communism still bewails its failure to eliminate religious practices and religious beliefs. The atheistic press continues to plan new strategies, new methods, new approaches. These frustrations and complaints, these new strategies are indeed a self-indictment—an admission of failure. The heritage of faith received through Sts. Cyril and Methodius has endured through eleven centuries, and has survived over a half-century the intensive effort of militant atheism.

Militant atheism has not – will not – cannot succeed

Because atheistic communism attempts to do violence to God's plan for the universe, because it attempts to do violence to the dignity and the inviolable rights with which God endowed man, it is certainly doomed to failure. Atheistic communism has inflicted serious wounds and sufferings, but it has not, will not and cannot succeed. Its eventual failure is a certainty beyond any doubt—beyond any question. The only question that begs an answer is: "How long will it continue to oppress and to inflict suffering upon innocent people? How long will it resist the natural aspiration of man for freedom?" We lack the charisma of prophecy. We cannot see into the future. However, we do not ignore the facts and the signs of the past and the present.

It is generally admitted today that Karl Marx's analysis of capitalism and his program to eliminate it are anachronistic—simply out of date. A few weeks ago some Italian communist leaders described Marxism as antiquated and irrelevant to the conditions of the modern industrial society. Marx was not aware of the possibility of automation, which has made such tremendous changes in production. He was not aware of atomic power. He was not aware of the potentials of our massive bulldozers or even of our helicopters that can place a church steeple or an air condenser in a fraction of the time and at a fraction of the cost that would otherwise be required. The Marxist program has lost its force, because the function and social position of the working classes has undergone such considerable changes that in many areas it does not differ from the function and position attributed to the bourgeoisie.

Violent suppression of freedom

Reviewing the past we know of the progressive erosion of international sympathy. The violence of the Bolshevik October Revolution disclosed the violent and unidealistic nature of the movement. It disclosed how little value communism places on human life. This was further highlighted by the mass starvation, which in the judgment of Stalin was required to enhance the communist program. The Moscow trials of the 30's; the Hitler-Stalin pact of 1939; the cruelties of the Soviet labor camps; the armed invasion and occupation under the guise of liberation of so many countries following the war; the 1956 armed intervention in Hungary; the Kremlin's role in Vietnam and the Middle East; and the tragic armed invasion of Czechoslovakia — all betray an effort to turn back the clock — a reversion to the blatant imperialism of the Czars.

Perhaps more significant than anything that has happened recently was the long-planned Unity Summit Conference of Communist Countries. After five years of careful planning and preparation, the Conference was boycotted by six of the fourteen communist parties in power. Another eight were deliberately absent. Of the seventy-five attending, only twenty were substantial and significant. Even some of those attending refused to subscribe to the so-called Brezhnev doctrine of limited sovereignty. Some insisted on communism by popular consent, an ideal forcefully resisted on the grounds that communism by popular consent would not be communism at all. Some of those attending criticized the proposed unity doctrine as irrelevant and utopian, and ridiculed the idea of a single Communist World Movement.

The Kremlin felt the need and tried vainly to justify the armed invasion of Czechoslovakia by proposing the doctrine of limited sovereignty—of the sphere of influence. If the latter is an admissible norm of international life, why are communist activities in Cuba and South America subsidized? Why are the Chinese activities on its eastern border—its sphere of influence—denounced? Since by charter and by proclamation the Kremlin is committed to world communism, does such a global goal place the entire world in its own sphere of influence? Would this mean that the Kremlin alone has absolute sovereignty with the right of armed invasion and occupation of any nation in the world?

Progressively, the Kremlin gives stronger evidence that its system is incompatible with basic human freedoms. More and more it must resort to military power to perpetuate itself. More and more the Kremlin provides evidence that it is but a carbon copy of the very imperialism which it denounces. More and more it demonstrates that it is not a government of the people, by the people, or for the people.

Soviet communism gives increasing evidence of its determination to violate the will of God and the sacred rights of persons, and of the family of nations. Force is used to suppress the basic freedom of religion to which man is entitled by his dignity as a human person, and without which no other freedom can survive.

Today, as we honor the apostles of the Slavs, we fervently pray to them with the conviction that they are not only interested, but they are also powerful intercessors in behalf of the suffering Slavic peoples. Through their intercession, we beg God to give the oppressed Slavic peoples the courage to continue their witness to the heritage of faith. We beg God that the vein of gold—the tradition of faith and the spiritual values that form the heritage received through Sts. Cyril and Methodius—may continue to endure and to influence the lives of our suffering brothers. We pray that they may recover the freedom to which they are justly entitled. We pray that their suffering and long agony may soon see the bright dawn of resurrection. This is our fervent prayer today. These are the petitions which, through the intercession of Sts. Cyril and Methodius, we send up to Almighty God through Christ our Lord. Amen.

Peace — an Enterprise of Justice Among Nations

Address at the Memorial Service of the National Convention of Veterans of Foreign Wars, on August 17, 1969.

"Those who are pledged to the service of their country as members of its armed forces should regard themselves as agents of security and freedom.... They make a genuine contribution to the establishment of peace" (Vatican II, Pastoral Constitution on the Church in the Modern World, no. 79).

In this City of Brotherly Love — the cradle of our nation's independence — we are assembled at this Memorial Service of the National Convention of the Veterans of Foreign Wars. We meet to give prayerful witness to the VFW motto: "Honor the dead by serving the living."

We pay tribute to the memory and pray for the immortal souls of all your deceased comrades. Gratefully conscious of their contribution to our own freedom and security and to the cause of peace, we pay special tribute to those who gave the last full measure of their devotion — their mortal life — in the service of their country.

Our gratitude impels us for their sake, so that they will not have died in vain, and for our own sake, so that we may be spared the horrors of a nuclear war, to rededicate ourselves to the cause of world peace. No greater honor can we pay to your fallen comrades, and no greater service can we render to the living, than by declaring an all-out war against war, and by a determined dedication to the task of promoting peace and justice among nations. We must enlist the energies and encourage the arduous and unceasing efforts of all men of good will in promoting instruments of peace and in outlawing all wars.

World peace is not a vain hope. It can be achieved with diligent effort and can be preserved with constant vigilance. It is man who makes war. It is man who must make peace. Man must live and act with the conviction that international controversies can be resolved by reason; by negotiations founded on law, justice and equity. Peace is an enterprise of justice. It cannot be built and maintained by violence. Peace demands mutual trust and confidence, coupled with a determination to respect the rights and dignity of other persons and peoples and to cooperate with them in the pursuit of the shared hopes of mankind.

Peace is not pacifism

The Gospel message centered on love is at heart a doctrine of non-violence rather than violence. Jesus rejected the use of violence in His defense, yet He found Himself in conflict with the lawful authorities who condemned Him to death on the cross. He was the Prince of Peace who came to cast a fire upon the earth, and to bring a sword — conflict — even within the framework of families (cf. Mt. 10:34). Jesus describes the life of a Christian in terms of warfare, and Paul illustrates the apostolate in terms of military service — a good soldier of Christ, fighting the good fight. The Gospel does not give a moral repudiation of war and violence, but simply points to its futility. Jesus does not prescribe a total abolishment of war, but He affirms that it destroys those who engage in it.

The message of the Gospel is a message of love and of a peace which the world cannot give. Peace is an enterprise of justice. It is also the fruit of love which goes beyond the requirements of justice. Peace cannot be invoked to protect disorder and injustice. It cannot be invoked to give permanency and respectability to the violation of human rights and human dignity.

The right and duty to provide for the common defense cannot be denied. Insofar as men are sinful, the threat of war hangs over them. As long as the danger of war remains, governments cannot be denied the right to legitimate defense once every means of peaceful settlement has been exhausted. The right of legitimate defense — as a last resort — was affirmed by the Second Vatican Council as operating within the limits of the natural and evangelical law (Pastoral Constitution on the Church in the Modern World, no. 79).

Peace proclaims the highest and most universal values of life: truth, justice, freedom and love. In this context, Pope Paul VI said that peace does "not favor the cowardice of those who fear it may be their duty to give their life for the service of their own country and of their own brothers, when these are engaged in the defense of justice and liberty..." (Dec. 15, 1967). The desire for peace is not a justification for cowardice. It is a demand for courage.

If war is to be outlawed and replaced by more humane and enlightened methods of regulating conflicts among nations, it will be because citizens insisted on principles of non-violent action. In this context, *conscientious objection* deserves the legal provisions made for it. Such provisions, now accorded to those whose reasons are grounded on total rejection of the use of military force, should be extended to make it possible, although not easy, for so-called *selective-conscientious objectors*. Such persons should be excused from serving in wars which they consider unjust, or in branches of service—such as strategic nuclear forces—which would subject them to the performance of actions contrary to deeply and sincerely held convictions about indiscriminate killing. Such persons should be required to render some other form of service to the human community.

The appeal to conscience is not only valid, but necessary. It will be a determining factor in the establishment of a universal peace. In his address to the United Nations, Pope Paul said, "Today, in an era marked by such human progress, there is need for an appeal to the moral conscience of man. For the danger comes, not from progress, nor from science.... The real danger comes from man himself, who has at his disposal ever more powerful instruments, which can be used for destruction as well as for the loftiest conquests."

The arms race

The arms race is an utterly treacherous trap for humanity. Acknowledging the right of governments to legitimate self-defense, and the constitutional duty of our own government "to provide for the common defense," we repeat the clear warning of the Fathers of the Second Vatican Council that the arms race is an utterly treacherous trap for humanity which injures the poor to an intolerable degree (Pastoral Constitution on the Church in the Modern World, no. 81).

The arms race does not insure a lasting peace. The strategic balance of power or of terror it produces does not eliminate the threat of war. It merely increases the threat of greater and more devastating wars. One nuclear exchange between the United States and the Soviet Union would claim as much and possibly more than 120 million American lives. Is the risk of so many lives an adequate provision for common defense?

Recent disclosures about our nation's military defense program and budget make us recall, with sobering reflection, the words of our great general and late President, Dwight D. Eisenhower. In his farewell address, he said: "In the councils of government we must guard against the acquisition of unwarranted influence by the military-industrial complex.... We must never let the weight of this combination endanger our liberties or democratic processes. We should take nothing for granted. Only an alert and knowledgeable citizenry can compel the proper meshing of the huge industrial and military machinery of defense with our peaceful methods and goals, so that security and liberty may prosper forever."

These words, spoken by one of our eminent citizens, who was qualified to speak from military and political experience, raise the haunting question as to whether our program of national defense may not itself be a threat to our national security—to our national destiny. It raises the question of whether by allotting 77½ out of the $178.9 billion 1968 budget, we are making adequate provisions "to form a more perfect union" by eliminating social and economic inequities. It raises the question as to whether by allotting such a minor percentage to the purpose of "establishing justice and ensuring domestic tranquility" we are neglecting those whom we are defending. Our military budget rises each year, spurred on by a seemingly self-generating mechanism.

Recently we read about the ABM (antiballistic missile) controversy. Though these are purely defensive, yet their build-up—whether thick or thin—upsets the strategic balance of terror, and provides an excuse to expand the escalation of the arms race. The ABM controversy gave cause to seriously question the policy of maintaining nuclear superiority; to question whether it is truly meaningful for security.

Now that the Safeguard ABM battle is over, a more critical debate is about to begin over the testing of offensive MIRV (multiple independently targeted re-entry vehicles) multiple warhead missiles. Flight tests of these missiles raise the further question of whether the point of no return has not been passed, opening an era of a five-fold multiplication of delivery vehicles in the American strategic offensive missile forces. We may expect that the promotional approach will follow the normal pattern, viz., that we must have superiority even for purposes of negotiation in the strategic arms limitation talks (SALT).

The defense spending from 1959 to 1968 exceeded $551 billion dollars. This amount was twice as much as was spent by the Federal, state and local governments for education. Not only the amount spent for defense is cause for grave concern, but the methods in which these funds are spent raise the question about the threat of the military-industrial complex. When after World War II the Armed Services Procurement Act was passed, allowing for the so-called negotiated contracts, President Truman noted that the Act gave "unprecedented freedom" and created the danger of "excessive placement of contracts by negotiation and undue reliance upon large concerns, and this must not occur."

The issue is not the right and the need for a program of defense. The issue is whether the program and budget for defense is being carried to the extreme of being itself a threat to our national security. Loyal citizens have a right and duty to raise such questions when $77.4 billion are allotted to defense and less than $70 billion (excluding interest on the national debt) is allotted to civilian needs. Of this, $2 billion was allotted to federal housing; $2 billion to the poverty program; and $5.2 billion to the education program.

In this frame of reference, we quote again from the farewell address of President Eisenhower: "Disarmament with mutual honor and confidence is a continuing imperative. Together we must learn how to compose differences not with arms, but with intellect and decent purpose."

Christian morality is not lacking in realism. Vatican Council II called for reciprocal or collective disarmament proceeding at an equal pace according to agreement backed up by authentic and workable safeguards.

Directing all efforts towards peace

Peace cannot be reduced solely to the maintenance of a balance of power between enemies. Peace is an enterprise of justice that must be built up ceaselessly. We must develop new attitudes in promoting peace. We must, above all, encourage arduous and unceasing efforts of statesmen and specialists in the fields of arms control and disarmament. We must encourage peacemaking and peacemaking machinery. We must work for a stronger and more effective United Nations so that it will become a true instrument of peace and justice among nations.

I speak to you, the veterans of foreign wars, because you, above all, know the horrors of war and the value of peace. You have demonstrated your loyalty and devotion to your country. By your military service you were making a contribution toward world peace.

May I recall that world peace is not a vain hope; that peace is not pacifism; that the right of legitimate self-defense cannot be questioned, and that no one can question the need of an effective defense program. However, unless greater efforts are made toward negotiations for arms control and disarmament, we face the grave danger of destroying our national security and destiny by our escalating program of military defense.

You can pay no greater honor to your fallen comrades than by directing all your efforts toward the promotion of the peace for which they fought and died. You can render no greater service to the living than to promote peaceful cooperation in the entire family of nations....

The truly committed Christian knows... beyond the shadow of a doubt... and after centuries of human experience that peace can come only when there is universal respect for life. Respect for life *in all stages of existence:* respect for the *right of the unborn to the life which is already theirs;* respect for life in the womb, in the hospital ward, in a home for the elderly, or in a war-torn land.

Peace will come to the world when the basic rights to life, to education, to the opportunity to work, and to live in a decent home are established for all; when the loneliness that grips the lives of the elderly, the isolation of decaying urban centers, and injustices toward minority groups are overcome.

The call of our commitment to Christ is a call to apply the Gospel principles of justice to the problems of the day, and to do so before the problems erupt in bitterness, anger, and violence. It is a call to return to Christ, and through Him, with Him, and in Him, to seek to do His will.

To Insure Peace Man Must Acknowledge God

Acceptance of the 25th Anniversary Gold Medal Public Service Award from the Philadelphia Public Relations Association, on May 27, 1970.

Esteemed Guests and Members of the Philadelphia Public Relations Association:

...On this 25th anniversary of the founding of your Association, I offer to you my sincere congratulations, and invite you to reflect on some other important events that occurred in that same year—1945.

We greeted the new year 1945 with fatigue. We were in the fifth year of the global World War II, and we were reeling from its increasing fury. We desired peace. We prayed for it, and we fought with the conviction that total victory would bring peace.

In the first quarter of 1945 there was a rapid succession of events. The start of massive air raids on Tokyo was followed by the invasion of Iwo Jima and later Okinawa. In March, the last of the V-rockets fell on Britain. In April, President Roosevelt died, Mussolini was killed by the partisans, and the death of Hitler was reported. Atom bombs dropped on Hiroshima and Nagasaki on August 6th and 9th, and were followed by Japan's surrender on August 14th, and with it the end of World War II.

The Yalta and Potsdam Conferences in February and July determined the terms of the surrender and the reapportionment of Europe into spheres of interest and control. Millions of people in different nations were "liberated" into the Kremlin camp of captive and controlled nations. In the same year, the Independent Vietnam Republic with Ho Chi Minh as President was formed. The rupture between Chiang Kai-shek and Mao Tse-tung led to the continuing conflict between Chinese Communists and Nationalists. Egypt, Iraq, Syria and Lebanon served notice that the creation of a Jewish state in Palestine would lead to war. The Arab League was founded. In December, the Foreign Ministers of Britain, the United States and the USSR met in Moscow to form a provisional government in Korea.

In the same year of 1945, the atom bomb—a product of our laboratories—added frightening dimensions of destructive power to wars, and the United Nations Charter—a product of our national experience—was established as an international effort to restrain and control such power.

We prayed fervently for the end of World War II. We welcomed that end with unrestrained joy and with the conviction that peace would ensue. Upon reflection, however, we can now see that the end of the war was attended by certain events which contained the seed of new conflicts—including those in Indochina and in the Middle East.

The events of 1945, viewed in a quarter of a century perspective, evince that military power can win a war, but it has failed to secure peace. Even the United Nations—an organized international effort—has not thus far achieved a lasting peace. What is the solution? Where do we look for an answer? The answer is as simple as its implementation is difficult. It is man who makes war! It is man who must make peace.

Need for a spiritual influence

Man's continued discovery of the secrets of nature is not matched by his discovery of his own spiritual nature. Man's increasing control of the forces about him is not matched by the control of the forces within him. Pope Paul told the United Nations: "The real danger comes from man himself who has at his disposal ever more powerful instruments, which can be used for destruction as well as for lofty conquests." Man must destroy the instruments of death or be destroyed by them.

In a similar vein, the editorialist, David Lawrence, wrote: "We must find a way to disarm the belligerency of man himself.... We turn to moral force...as the hopeful alternative to military force.... What we need in the world is a spiritual influence...a spiritual rebirth of man-responsible individualism.... This is nothing else than the responsibility of man to God Himself" (*U.S. News & World Report*, June 1, 1970—reprint from issue of June 14, 1957).

Faith is indeed a necessary condition for peace. Without faith—without a sense of responsibility to God—peace is impossible. Peace is the work of justice, given life and direction by charity. These two moral ingredients of peace are rooted in man's divine origin and in the equality of his nature. The solidarity of the human family and of the international community rests ultimately on the brotherhood of men under the fatherhood of God. We cannot deny or ignore God without denying the one necessary bond which makes all men brothers. If God and His order in the world are denied, there can be no law which would bind the international community.

To achieve and preserve peace, man must acknowledge God. He must acknowledge his dependence upon and responsibility to God. He must also acknowledge that there is a necessary and knowable order in the world which God has placed under the control and management of man. The history of mankind proves that there is no substitute for God's blueprint for world order: there is no instant or miracle formula for peace.

Peace demands courage

Peace is not a vain hope, nor a sentimental dream. It is a philosophy of action. Man must live and act with the conviction that international affairs are neither self-regulatory, nor beyond control; that international controversies can be resolved by negotiations based on mutual trust, confidence and willingness to forgive; that such negotiations must respect the rights and dignity of persons and peoples, and must enlist their cooperation in the pursuit of the shared hopes of mankind.

Peace should not be equated with pacifism, nor can it be invoked to protect discord, injustice, or the violation of human rights or human dignity. Peace demands the courage to substitute moral strength for brute force; the courage to undertake risks and sacrifices for the common good of the human family; the courage to redirect the minds of men to God, who in the Old Testament was called Yahweh-Shalom—God is Peace; and His Son in the New Testament was identified as the Prince of Peace—His Gospel was "the Gospel of Peace."

Today, a gratifying increase in the awareness of the urgent need for peace is matched by a diversity of views on how peace is to be attained. Such diversity, if reasoned and restrained, can be profitable. It is no tragedy to have hawks and doves; hard-hats and long-haired dissenters; the impatient young and the determined old; interventionists and hardened isolationists; those who would abandon smaller nations to imperialistic aggression and enslavement, and those who consider the defense of such nations as the first line of defense of our own nation. In our nuclear age, with its jet system of travel and communication, there is an interdependence among nations which does not permit any nation to turn its back on the rest of the world without hurting itself.

It is good that the young are interested and articulate and that "Solons" defend their convictions. We should not exaggerate the age gap.

The world has always been peopled by young and old. Neither has a monopoly on wisdom, vision or courage. Neither is omniscient or infallible. The cause of peace needs the wisdom, knowledge and experience of the old as urgently as it needs the vision, the courage and the daring of the young. Both must work together in patience, in faith and in mutual trust. Order cannot be achieved through disorder. Peace cannot be achieved through violence—on the battle front or on the home front.

God and His blueprint

The first rung of the ladder to peace is the spiritual rebirth of man. David Lawrence labels this as "responsible individualism" and defines it in the words: "This is nothing less than the responsibility of man to God Himself." Without such a sense of responsibility, military victories, international laws and treaties, and even the laudable efforts of the United Nations, will avail little.

As members of the Public Relations Association you may well appreciate the delicate and formidable task of religious leaders. Working in the sphere of our special competence, and always keeping a proper balance between the sacred and the secular, we must provide men and society with a light and a leaven—a knowledge of God, and His blueprint for individuals and for the world. We must help men to develop a sense of personal responsibility to God which must serve as a norm for all human action.

In an age when some writers are reviving the "God dead" theory, we must explain that light exists even though it is not seen by a blind man; that sound exists even though it is not heard by a deaf man; that the full beauty of stained glass windows is not seen from without, but from within the church. We must show that God is alive and that His commandments, even though disregarded or violated, do exist and do bind all human beings.

Since apostolic times, there has been a tendency to fashion a secular or world religion; to accept some of the tenets of the Gospel and to ignore or reject others. Truth is one and indivisible. The presentation of the truth must be adjusted to the circumstances of time, place and persons. But truth and doctrine cannot be modified to please the listeners.

Since God is infinite and man is finite, there must be mysteries in religion. Truths revealed by God in the Scriptures are no less truths because they transcend human comprehension. Our teaching of religion, therefore, places a heavy demand upon the human mind—a demand for faith, a faith which must be lived and expressed in charity.

The teaching of religion, to be effective, also places a heavy demand upon the human will. It must echo our Lord's call to penitence; a call to self-discipline and self-denial; a call to the discipleship of the cross, which to the pagans was a sign of rebuke and reproach, but to the Christians is a symbol of victory. We must echo our Lord's call to a love which is demonstrated by the observance of the commandments, a love which calls for sacrifice. We must, time and again, repeat the "You shall not" of the commandments and of the Gospel.

The Church and Arms Limitation

Excerpt from the talk delivered to the Synod in Rome, on October 22, 1971.

...What can the Church do in a practical and positive way to retard and reverse the accumulation of armaments—to develop new attitudes and directions?

The Church does not exercise direct power over nations, over political and economic life within nations, nor over the military-industrial complex which promotes arms production. The mission of the Church is to teach the social principles of the Gospel, and apply those principles to existing nations.

The Church should find no difficulty in finding a benevolent audience. Reasonable men are opposed to wars and to the enormous taxes imposed for military expenses. The Church should find no trouble in convincing the audience that all the stockpiling of armaments did not preclude the 40 wars that have occurred since 1945, or that in the 5,560 years of recorded history, some 14,000 wars have taken place with only 292 years of peace.

The Church should be relentless in its efforts to shape public opinion, and to create a climate in which theology, and not technology, would give direction to the course of human events. Then men would understand why arms limitation is a necessary step to general disarmament, which is a prerequisite to international justice, in which men, convinced that the arms race is a treacherous trap and war a tragic folly, would direct their efforts and resources toward removing the cause of war — injustice.

In 1968 the Bishops' Conference of the United States issued an urgent call for international peace, and questioned the values of the policy of maintaining nuclear superiority. This voice, together with many others including the World Council of Churches, led to the ABM debate of 1969 — the ABM was in doubt for some time, and was approved by a margin of one vote. Since then, the percentage of increase of military expenditures has leveled off. Let the Church proceed proclaiming the Gospel tirelessly against efforts to develop new weapons of destruction. In this way, it will do what it can to remove the causes of war and serious injustices.

Religion — Essential to a True and Lasting Peace

Sermon at the White House on December 17, 1972.

Invitation to prayer

Lord God, Creator and Supreme Governor of the universe, we gather today to offer You praise and thanksgiving.

For our loved ones,
for the bread we eat,
for the roar of the sea,
for the silence of the night,
and for this land which You have blessed
with abundance — we praise You for all we
have, for what we are and have is from You.

We acknowledge Your presence among us today. Help us to free our minds and hearts from the many preoccupations which seek to displace You in our lives. Help us to avoid distractions as we hear Your word today. Cleanse our hearts from all vain thoughts so that we can focus all attention upon You. Enlighten our minds, strengthen our wills, and kindle our affections so that we may worthily and devoutly participate in this service, and offer You the praise You so justly deserve.

Lord, we have been weak in the past. We have sinned in failing to walk in the path marked for us. With sincere repentance, we beg forgiveness for our faults and iniquities. May Your healing word strengthen us for the duties ahead so that, guided by Your light, we may never stray from the path which leads to You.

"Immanuel – God with us"

"The Lord himself will give you the sign: the virgin shall be with child and bear a son and shall name him Immanuel [God with us]" (Is. 7:14).

"When all things were in quiet silence, and the night was in the midst of her course, Your eternal Word leaped down from heaven from Your royal throne."

In this season, when we commemorate the historic journey of the Son of God from heaven to earth to redeem the world He had made, it is appropriate that we have witnessed an historic journey of men from earth to the heavens to explore the world God has made. For if man is ever inclined to be forgetful of the existence of God, he need only to look up to see the splendor, the order and the vastness of a universe too complex to have just happened, too predictable to have been the product of chance, too beautiful to have been the effect of any mere blind necessity.

Who will ever forget that Christmas Eve when this nation's astronauts gazed at the earth from the vantage point of the moon, and recited for all the world to hear the first verses of Genesis: "In the beginning, God created the heavens and the earth"?

"In the beginning, God...." The recognition of God not only as the cause of the universe, but also as the source of human dignity, has always been a principle of American life, a principle which this worship service illustrates and confirms.

As we salute the flag, we do not honor a State which recognized no authority beyond itself; we pledge allegiance to the symbol and to the reality of "one nation *under* God." Our coinage carries the reminder that our faith resides not in the material things which money represents, not in the gross national product, but that it is "in God we trust." The Declaration of our Independence as a nation articulates the principle that human rights are not the gift of a State which can rescind them at will; rather, human rights are the endowments of a Creator who has lavished on man gifts of life and liberty which mere human authority cannot rescind nor confiscate.

Thus, explicit in American principle and practice has been the recognition of God as the origin of human existence, the ultimate authority in human life and the destiny of human aspiration. The Supreme Court of the United States summarized this attitude well when it stated: "We are a religious people."

While sensitive to the principle of Church-State separation, this nation's highest tribunal has also been sensitive to the necessary connection between religion and life—a connection recognized in the constitutional guarantee of religion's free exercise.

Religion is indeed essential to human life. Without religion, man lacks an accurate awareness of his own place in the universe he so eagerly explores; without religion, man lacks an accurate assessment of the dignity he so eagerly claims. One need only examine the gray, spiritless effects of atheistic societies to observe the tangible results of human communities which seek to exclude God; and one need only look to the heroic spirit of faith which enlivens entire populations subject to godless governments to be inspired by the example of human communities from which God cannot be excluded.

But the message of religion is more than one of mere knowledge; it is a communication of love. Religion is not merely a question of facts to be recognized; it is a matter of truths to be lived. The nature of those truths of love, of recognition and of compassion is beautifully explained in the prophetic utterance of Isaiah as he describes the task of the Messiah:

"The Lord has anointed me, on me his spirit has fallen; he has sent me to bring the Good News to men that are humbled, to heal broken hearts, promising the release of captives, the opening of prison doors, proclaiming the year of the Lord's pardon, the day when he, our God, will give us redress."

For us to profess faith in God without hastening to eliminate the indignities inflicted upon men would be but empty rhetoric; for us to profess love of God without manifesting concern for the poor, the weak, and the lonely would be a caricature of religion.

In this context, it is appropriate to offer a silent prayer for all persons killed and maimed in war, for all prisoners of war, for those missing in action, and for all their families. May theirs be among the prison doors which are opened; may theirs be the wounded hearts which are healed; and may they be the special objects of God's love, and our continued concern.

A message of love

The distinctive message of God in Scripture, in both the Old and New Testaments, is a message of love. And our response to that message must be a response of love — not only love of God but also love of neighbor, for the two loves are essentially linked to form a single reality.

Is not the Psalmist's prophetic description of the love of the Messiah a moving example of the love all of us should show for others?

"He will give the poor redress when they cry to him, destitute folk, with none to befriend them; in their need and helplessness, they shall have his compassion."

And the fruit of such love, the Psalmist says, is a pledge which sounds as if it had been written today:

"Justice in his days shall thrive, and the blessings of peace; and may those days last till the moon shines no more."

True and lasting peace — for which we especially pray today — is thus the work of justice and of love — a justice which recognizes in each human being the image of God, and which recognizes each life as precious in God's sight; a love which realizes that God has first loved us, and which is willing to extend forgiveness in imitation of God.

And this manifestation of justice and love must not be limited to one nation, to one continent or to one hemisphere; it must be universal; it must be peace on earth. For when men deliberately isolate themselves or lock themselves into closed societies, they become narrow, selfish, and suspicious. It is no mere coincidence that it was the murderer of Abel who proposed the question: "Am I my brother's keeper?" We are all our brothers' keepers, not in the condescending sense of distrustful watchfulness, but in the charitable sense of fraternal concern. But a true interest in our brothers will be lacking unless we truly recognize that we have the same Father, God. We cannot speak of the family of man without acknowledging the Fatherhood of God.

Acknowledging God's authority, love and will

After asking by what name the Messiah would be known, the prophet Isaiah listed four titles — the last of which is "Prince of Peace." Implicit in this title is the essence of religion: a recognition of the authority of God; an acknowledgment of the love of God; an acceptance of the will of God.

The authority of God is recognized in the title of Prince; the love of God is acknowledged in the gift of peace; and the will of God is accepted in both the recognition of His authority, and in the acknowledgment of His gift.

This three-pillared religious foundation has been and must continue to be an acknowledged basis of American society. The authority of God is recognized in the title of Creator with which our Declaration of Independence describes Him; the love of God is acknowledged in that same document's recognition of the endowments He has given man and in the celebration of that day which most closely approaches a national holyday, Thanksgiving. The will of God is acknowledged in the meticulous care which we take to respect human rights, because this is a recognition both of God's transcendent authority, and of His generous love.

Within the lifetime of most of us here, we have seen the effects of the repudiation of God as the foundation of human society.

Less than two months ago, I stood at an altar in Oswiecim, Poland—better known to the world as Auschwitz—and I prayed for those who had died as the victims of an idealogy which recognized neither divine authority nor human rights. It is estimated that four million people died at Auschwitz alone, and the smoke still rises symbolically from the ruined ovens to which their bodies were consigned.

I saw the display cases with the hair clipped from the heads of those to be executed; cases with eyeglass frames snatched from the faces of those who had to grope their way to their death; cases with the clothing ripped from the bodies of infants unwanted or considered unworthy to live.

The most important law of God was trampled — the law that "You Shall Love." And when individuals look upon their fellow human beings and fail to see their humanity, it is often because they have turned their eyes from God, and have failed to acknowledge His divinity. The law of love is essentially one, but its expression is twofold: "You shall love the Lord your God with your whole heart, with your whole soul, and with your whole mind"; "You shall love your neighbor as yourself." This is not two laws but one law — indivisible and inseparable — the single and sovereign law of love.

At Auschwitz this was forgotten. May God grant that it will not be forgotten again. May God grant that the precious right to life may never be subordinated to political, economic, or personal expediency or whims.

And so I placed fresh flowers at the marker which commemorated the millions of Jews who died in that horrible place; and I offered special prayers for my fellow priests who had been executed there and in other Nazi death camps.

But in those rites, I also joined with almost half a million people who had walked in the rain to pay honor to a man — a priest — Blessed Maximilian Kolbe, who died as a victim of injustice, but who died loving his enemies and praying for their forgiveness. He freely offered his life in exchange for the life of another — and he expressed no bitterness, no recrimination; only forgiveness and love.

In the face of such heroism, who is truly the conqueror, and who are the conquered? We cannot despair at the apparent power of philosophies which reject divine law and human dignity when we see them disintegrate in the face of faith and forgiveness. But we must not let our own philosophy become godless; we must not forget our own dignity and our own destiny as children of God; and we must not be afraid to love and to forgive.

But we cannot love unless we know; and we know little of man if we know nothing of God; we know much about man if we know something about God; and we know that every man is our brother when we are ready to admit that God is our Father. This truth is the guarantee of our life and the foundation of our liberty. This truth about the reality of God is to be the focal point of our lives.

And is not this season an appropriate time for bringing into clearer focus this all-important and preeminent truth—the truth that God indeed lives, and that He truly loves us? Isn't the birth of the promised Messiah, Jesus Christ of Bethlehem, truly an affirmation of the sacred name Immanuel, "God with us"? And is not His message nothing more than the anticipation of the highest hopes of our century—unity and universality, peace and brotherhood, the nobility and salvation of man, love and freedom for every man?

It is this conviction of God's sovereign power and abiding presence, this conviction of "God with us," which motivated our fathers and continues to inspire us today.

When Columbus discovered this hemisphere 480 years ago, he planted the symbol of his faith on the shores of a new land; when the astronauts circled the moon, they broadcast a summary of their faith across the vastness of space.

The greatest achievements and the most noble moments in the history of our new world have been accompanied by the reaffirmation of an eternal truth:

"In the beginning, God...."

He is the origin of our existence, the source of our dignity, the reality of our destiny. In His will is our peace.

Final blessing

Lord, we thank You for these moments we have spent with You. We beseech You, grant us diligence in seeking You, a way of life that is pleasing to You, and perseverance that waits for You.

Protect us with Your power; enlighten us with Your wisdom; lead us with Your light so that, in the days to come, Your will may be done on earth as it is in heaven.

May the commemoration of our Lord's coming from heaven to earth fill us with an abundance of joys and blessings; deepen our awareness that God is with us; strengthen our determination to please Him in all things and to attain everlasting reward for deeds well done, and for a life well lived. Amen.

Statement on Abortion

Issued from Washington, NCCB, January 22, 1973.

The Supreme Court's decision today is an unspeakable tragedy for this nation. It is hard to think of any decision in the 200 years of our history which has had more disastrous implications for our stability as a civilized society. The ruling drastically diminishes the constitutional guarantee of the right to life, and in doing so sets in motion developments which are terrifying to contemplate.

The ruling represents bad logic and bad law. There is no rational justification for allowing unrestricted abortion up to the third month of pregnancy. The development of life before and after birth is a continuous process, and in making the three-month point the *cutoff* for unrestricted abortion, the court *seems* more impressed by magic than by scientific evidence regarding fetal development. The child in the womb has the right to the life it already possesses, and this is a right no court has authority to deny.

Apparently, the Court was trying to straddle the fence and give something to everybody: abortion on demand before three months for those who want that; somewhat more restrictive abortion regulations after three months for those who want that. But in its straddling act, the Court has done a monstrous injustice to the thousands of unborn children whose lives may be destroyed as a result of this decision.

No court and no legislature in the land can make something evil become something good. Abortion at any stage of pregnancy is evil. This is not a question of sectarian morality, but instead concerns the law of God and the basis of civilized society. One trusts in the decency and good sense of the American people not to let an illogical Court decision dictate to them on the subject of morality and human life.

United Against Godless Ideologies

Presentation at the Colloquium on the Holocaust, on April 11, 1973.

In this session, attention is focused on the sources of European Nihilism.

What is Nihilism?

Nihilism, as a 19th century Russian intellectual movement, matured under Czarist absolution, and was expressed in a program of revolutionary reform and terrorism as a means of liberating man from any kind of social, political, and religious "oppression," and any sort of enslavement. It was popularized by Ivan Turgenev's novel *Fathers and Sons* (1862) and given full expression by its chief protagonists, Nikolai Chernishevsky; Nikolai Dobrolyubov and Dmitry I. Pisarev.

Materialism and atheism were both preconditions and logical consequences of Nihilist criticism and negation. Nihilists denied traditional values and beliefs; denied intrinsic value in life, and said all existence is senseless and useless. They denied any objective basis for truth, for moral principles and denied any objective basis for God, spirit, soul, state, church, nationality, or high culture. These negations provided a premise for Nihilist anarchism, and anticipated the atheistic-materialism of Bolshevism in Russia. The sources of Nihilism can be traced to the beginning of the modern era of philosophy in the 17th century. The traces are found in the treatises on man, on God, and man's ability to know objective truth and reality, and to know God through reason.

Rene Descartes (1596-1656), through a subtle but serious error introduced the principle of modern rationalism which within a century led to the divorce of faith and reason and to the eventual denial of faith in God. His principle of dualism made the subject rather than the object the norm of truth. He attributed reality not to the object external to man, but to man's internal conception of that object.

Spinoza (1632-1677) brought the Cartesian principles of Dualism by inflexible logic to its termination, resulting in rash confidence in pure reason — in a form of Pantheism and the negation of human liberty. Liebnitz (1646-1716) developed rationalism into a theory of psychological determinism. Hobbes (1588-1679) went so far as to say that, in times of war, force and fraud are two cardinal virtues. He claimed that religion and Church is but a civil society, over which the civil sovereign had supreme authority in matters of cult and belief.

French philosophers abandoned the spiritualistic and metaphysical propositions of Cartesianism in favor of Mechanism and Materialism. David Hume (1711-1776) adopted the theory of Phenomenalism and claimed that God's existence and providence were irremediably inaccessible to all sciences, and hence no religion is speculatively justifiable.

Kant (1724-1804) adopted a theory of knowledge in which reason is autonomous and imposes its laws on reality. By means of the categorical imperative, he said that practical reason formulates a fundamental, synthetic *a priori* judgment which is the supreme principle conferring a moral value on all particular laws. Kant's great weakness was his failure to justify knowledge of the *thing-in-itself*.

Hegel (1770-1831), an idealist and a subjective, tried to explain the nature of the world in the light of eternity. He identified pure reason with the Diety itself; he could not defend personal immortality; he had to affirm everything, including war, violence, brutality as something good. He idealized the State, seeing it as the March of God in the world. He contributed much to the belief in the almighty power of the State — which had to be accepted with all its conditions and weaknesses. His philosophy of world history was a prototype of Nietzsche's ideology of power. While some considered him as a Theistic thinker, and others saw him as a Pantheist, David Strauss, Ludwig Feuerbach, Karl Marx and Friedrich Engels considered him atheistic and developed his thoughts into complete materialism.

Friedrich W. Nietzsche (1844-1900) was a Lebensphilosoph castigating the separation of philosophy and science from life. He diagnosed Historicism and Scientism as symptoms of decadence and of a Nihilism that threatened the foundations of Western civilization. He called for a new beginning and a transvaluation of all values in order to stop such threats. He launched a radical attack on traditional theology, Metaphysics and morality. With Feuerbach, he saw the idea of God and absolute truth as nothing but projections of man's most precious qualities into an illusory beyond—qualities which must be reclaimed for the enrichment of man in his "this worldly" existence. He solemnly dramatized the *Death of God* in the story of the "Madman" in section 125 of *Die Frohliche Wissenschaft*. He implemented his early thinking with the deadly theory of *Biological and Social Darwinism*. The "World Ground" he saw as *Wille Zue Macht*— a "Will to Power"— that by sublimation would generate the *Super Man*.

In his *The Genealogy of Morals*, he held the Jews responsible for the birth of Christian "slave morality" according to which the wretched, the poor, the weak, the lowly, the suffering, the sick, the loathsome are the only ones who are pious, blessed and sure of salvation. He wrote of the "*Blond Beast*"—the noble product of the masterful race—the superior man who comes into being as the result of murders, arson, torture, and rape.

The ambivalence and self-contradictory theses in Nietzsche's thinking account for some gross misrepresentations of his philosophy. Though the National Socialists attributed to him their anti-Semitism, Nietzsche gave a scathing denunciation of racism and of the power politics and crude materialism of the German Empire. He formulated no new table of values, but devaluated existing values. He did not master Nihilism but rather was mastered by it. His was a sick mind which succeeded only in negating. He fostered the rise of irrationalism, subjectivism, voluntarism, and a biologism based on the *elan vital* of a naturalistic Lebensphilosophic. Shortly before becoming deranged, he wrote the *ecce homo* in which he predicted his own greatness as a man of destiny, saying that "politics on a grand scale will date me.... Some day my name will be bound up with the recollection of something terrific."

Richard Wagner (1813-1883), a composer and theorist of music fame, was a pseudo-philosophic writer. He conceived a dream world populated by a purified, redeemed humanity unfettered by law or religious dogma. His was a Faustian distillation of all the influences he had absorbed from other philosophers including Nietzsche's "Will to Power" and the anarchism of his fellow revolutionary, Bakunin.

Charles Darwin (1809-1882), an undisguised agnostic, developed the theory of natural selection and evolution. His theory was developed by Herbert Spencer (1820-1903). According to his notion of transfigured realism, truth is "the accurate correspondence of subjective to objective relations." He did not acknowledge freedom of the will and hence for him traditional morality lost its significance. He defined morality as "the deduction of the more and more perfect forms which human action, whether individual or social, *necessarily adopts,* subject to the fundamental law of evolution."

These and other philosophers and pseudo-philosophers exerted and influenced and in varying degrees must be regarded as the source of the theories and ideas which gave rise to European Nihilism as it was reflected in and practiced by National Socialism.

National Socialism

National Socialism was not a systematically developed or organized program, nor did it have a firmly constructed set of concepts or values. Neither the original twenty-five point program of the Nationalsozialistische Deutsche Arbeiterpartei formulated in 1920 by Gottfried Feder, nor Hitler's *Mein Kampf* (1925-6) nor the *Mythus Des 10 Jahrhunderts* (1930) of Alfred Rosenberg offered any politically, socially, culturally, or religiously grounded Weltanschauung. As an ideology, it lacked unity and had stark contradictions. It was in these respects in sharp contrast to Bolshevism.

National Socialism was a primitive mixture — for popular consumption — of extreme nationalism, social Darwinian Biologism, anti-Semitism with aggressive imperialism dedicated to the task of preserving the Nordic-Aryan race for the right to leadership, which was regarded as racially determined and assigned with adequate living space and even world domination to the Germanic "Master Race." Invoking Nietzsche's "Will to Power," National Socialism combined its claim to complete and sole power in the State with the demand that life should be radically reoriented toward permanent and complete mobilization for permanent war.

Christianity, described as "alien to the race," was to be replaced by a pseudo-religiosity designated as Gottglaubigkeit (belief in God). A conglomerate ideology was offered as a substitute religion. By affirming the undisguised cult of power and force as historically justified strength, National Socialism denied all moral values, and to the same extent revealed itself as pure Nihilism.

Hitler's militant ideological imagery was influenced by Richard Wagner's world—an ambiguous mixture of revolutionary, political, and artistic ambition. Hitler assimilated the extreme anti-Semitism associated with the Alldeutsche Group and George Von Schonerer and the concept of "Noble Race" taught by the religious sectarian Jorg Lanz Von Liebenfeld, who advocated a creed of racial purity. Lanz claimed to be the Father of Nazism, but in 1938 he was officially forbidden to write.

Hitler's demand for Lebensraum was to be satisfied at the expense of neighboring nations through emigration and annihilation. Nations would be isolated and singled out as the enemy race for exclusion from the international community. The myth of the enemy race was a counterpart to the Bolshevist myth of the enemy class. When in 1933 the vaguely defined content of National Socialism was applied as a political doctrine, it became a dangerous weapon. The one constant in this doctrine was hostility to the inferior race — which included the Jews.

Hitlerian Anti-Semitism

If light is to be shed on the spiritual roots of the Holocaust, the question must be raised whether Hiltlerian anti-Semitism was a new phase of an age-old demonry or whether it was a new variety of anti-Judaism.

The Scriptures introduce us to the persecution of the chosen people — by conquest, by exile and by oppression. Since the days of classical Greece, Jews have been persecuted by pagans, Christians, Moslems, atheists, and sometimes even by Jews. There are reasons to believe that the Hitlerian variety of anti-Judaism was somewhat different.

It should be recalled that the theory of race evolved in Germany from the Hegelian philosophy which characterized the Jews as a Semitic people — inferior, corrupting and unassimilable. The new Nationalist spirit could not tolerate the religio-ethnic independence nor the business prowess of the Jews. In 1870, Marx's pamphlet, *Victory of Judaism Over Germanism*, set off waves of reaction in Parliament, in universities and on the streets. (Catholic organ *Germania* was one of the first to condemn Jew-Baiting.) In France, the Jews were fingered as scapegoats in the loss of the war of 1870 and in the political scandals in Edouard Drumont's *La France Juive*, which went through one hundred editions. The 1905 pamphlet, *Protocols of the Elders of Zion*, became the Bible for anti-Semitism. In Russia the Bolshevik victory of 1917 had a constitutional ban on anti-Semitism. However, the prominent Jews in the Revolution were liquidated; the Jews were suspected of international conspiracy, and the constitutional guarantee was used as a device to wrest Jews from Judaism.

Hitler in 1933 called for a purge of Jews from all phases of German life. In 1935 the Nuremberg "Laws" stripped Jews of their citizenship. The wearing of the yellow badge was decreed two years later, and a cultural attack was launched to eliminate Jews from teaching, journalism, the theater, and labor organizations. A pogrom took place in 1938. On October 12, 1939, Hitler decreed the establishment of Jewish Councils—the *Judenrat*—of twenty-four members which were charged with the obligation of carrying out the orders of German official agencies. The strategy of the Germans was to engage the collaboration of the Council with the hope that the majority of Jews would be saved and the minority only would be sacrificed. The final solution, annihilation, seems to have been adopted in 1941. Jewish resistance—except for the Warsaw Ghetto uprising in which 25,000 Jews perished—was scant.

While some Jewish observers—Theodore Reinach, Heinrich Graetz, Jules Isaacs—and some non-Jewish—James Parkes and Rev. Paul Demann—regard the wave of anti-Semitism as a continuation of the old evil, others propose a different analysis. The irrational quality of Hitlerian anti-Judaism—which was directed more against race than religion—led Sigmund Freud, Maurice Samuel and Jacques Maritain to reduce the new anti-Semitism to a "Christophobia" — an unconscious hatred of Christianity which was projected on the Jews as cognates of Christianity's Founder. In an extension of this view to include pagan and neopagan anti-Semites, the Hitlerian anti-Semitism may be viewed as a "nomophobia" or unconscious and displaced resentment of all law or restraint. This extension is strengthened by Hitler's remark quoted by Hermann Rauschning: "Conscience — the Jewish invention." It would also be strengthened by the take-over of Austria and the Sudentenlands, inhabited predominantly by a Christian and Catholic population. A further strengthening of this theory is that as early as May, 1939, the invasion of Poland was considered for the purpose of totally eliminating the national identity of the people. Finally, the special targets of the Nazi invaders in Germany and in Poland were the clergy, a fact which is well documented in the book: *Priester vor Hitler's Tribunalen,* written by Benedicta Maria Kempner of Lansdowne, wife of one of the prosecutors in the Nuremberg Trials.

Lessons derived from the Holocaust

The subtle yet serious philosophical errors of Descartes, developed by other philosophers — some of whom have been mentioned above — led to departure from philosophical realism which held that the recognition of objective reality is impossible, and maintained that truth was to conform to man, rather than man conform to truth. If there is no possibility of knowing the existence of God through reason, then logically there is no possibility of knowing the inherent dignity of man, which is based on a recognition of God's reality. If there is no possibility of knowing man and God, then, of course, as so many of the modern philosophers allege, religion and morality have no validity. If this be so, then there are no valid restraints on the action of man, and even less on the actions of the State.

Yet religion is essential to human life. Without religion, man lacks an accurate awareness of his own place in the universe he so eagerly explores; without religion, man lacks an accurate assessment of the dignity he so eagerly claims. We cannot despair at the apparent power of philosophies which reject divine law and human dignity. But we must not let our own philosophy become godless; we must not forget our own dignity and our own destiny as children of God; and we must not be afraid to carry into effect the most important commandment of love of God and neighbor.

But we cannot love unless we know; and we know little of man if we know nothing of God; we know much about man if we know something about God, and we know that every man is our brother when we are ready to admit that God is our Father. This truth is the guarantee of our life and the foundation of our liberty.

Jewish legacy to humankind

In the Second World War, Poland lost fifteen of its thirty-five million people. About 10% of

Poland's population in 1939—or 3.5 million—was Jewish. At the Auschwitz Camp alone, about 4 million people died. Among the victims were Gypsies, Russians, Poles, Jews, Ukrainians, Czechs, and Slovaks, and even Germans. It is a documented fact that many Poles—who were never consigned to the concentration camps—were shot publicly in their own towns and villages for sheltering Jews.

Because attention is being focused in this Colloquium on the Holocaust as it relates to the Jews, perhaps it may help to review the benefactions of the Jewish people to humankind—benefactions which were negated through the philosophical developments which laid the foundations for the abuse of human dignity and the violation of human rights.

The first legacy of the Jewish people is their firm belief in God. This belief was the focal point of their culture and the thread that held all else in place. In their long history, all the Jews preserved—at times against hostile odds—their belief in God. Their Yahweh of the Scriptures was not a magnified human personality, but the Master of all creation, who had the right to impose His will upon man and history, and who insisted on moral rectitude as a precondition for divine worship. His commandments were not abstractions but specific directives spelling out the duties to neighbor in adequate detail with the effect that the Bible is the source of the first formulation of social justice.

A second legacy of the Jewish people is the doctrine of man's immense and incomparable dignity. This doctrine is best expressed by the psalmist, who, after contrasting man's finite nature with God's infinite majesty, extols the dignity and power to which God has raised man: "What is man that you should be mindful of him, or the son of man that you should care for him? You have made him little less than the angels and crowned him with glory and honor. You gave him rule over the works of your hands, putting all things under his feet" (8:5-7). This passage articulates the reality that God is the foundation to man's claim to incomparable dignity, to his immortal destiny and to his inviolable integrity.

A third legacy of the Jewish people is the doctrine of moral choice. God has given man mastery over his world through the divinely given capacity to "choose the good and reject the evil." This reality of man's freedom of choice contradicted the old pagan philosophies of fatalism, disguised by Marx under the name of economic determinism, and by others under the name of psychological determinism. This divergent outlook on man's freedom of choice is a principal cause of the radical and irreconcilable division between the free world and the world of communism today. This doctrine of moral choice carries with it social implications. The command "You shall love your neighbor as yourself" provides the concept of the solidarity in human relations, and the concept of a moral law applicable to societies as well as to individuals.

The Declaration of the Second Vatican Council on Non-Christian Religions averred the common patrimony of Christians with the Jews: "We are Abraham's sons according to the faith." In the words of Paul, the Church has drawn "sustenance from the root of that good olive tree [Israel] onto which have been grafted the wild olive branches of the Gentiles." It can be said that Jesus came from the deepest soul of Jewish history, and His Church was born out of Israel's loin.

This legacy of the Jewish people must be preserved if we are to survive as a free people. Our traditions, though different, are inextricably interwoven.

May I conclude this presentation with a question: How long will we permit an exploitation of our differences by the godless at the cost of submerging our common belief in God and in the incomparable dignity and spiritual destiny of man? Dare we through our divisions again open the way for the desecration of the human person and human life? God forbid that our failure to unite against godless ideologies should make another Belsen, another Dachau, or another Auschwitz possible!

A Timely Instrument To Communicate Timeless Truth

Statement on NC News Service Wire Transmission, on May 14, 1973.

For all who profess to be followers of Jesus Christ, the effective communication of vital truth is not an optional invitation but an essential mandate.

Jesus commanded His apostles to preach the good news of the Gospel, and to teach all nations. The apostles themselves understood that they were not fulfilling their responsibilities if they neglected this most important task.

The marketplace in which St. Paul preached, however, has been replaced by a forum which girdles the globe. It is now possible to preach the good news universally and to teach all nations simultaneously.

This world-wide forum, however, has not been addressed by Christ's followers as skillfully as it should have been. Ten years ago, on the feast of Sts. Peter and Paul, Pope Paul VI told newsmen that the Catholic press should emulate the technical excellence of the secular press if it is to compete with it in promoting the Faith as effectively as the secular press promotes its objectives. Only a few months later, in the first decree approved by the Second Vatican Council and promulgated by Pope Paul, the bishops of the world declared that the Church "judges it part of her duty to preach the news of redemption with the aid of the instruments of social communication."

The inauguration of this wire transmission system by the National Catholic News Service provides the Church with a timely instrument for communicating timeless truth. As justice delayed is justice denied, so truth delayed has often been truth distorted—since even heroic follow-up efforts have almost never been able to overcome misconceptions caused by some reports in the secular press which lacked either accuracy in content or completeness in context. This transmission system is thus in the service of truth, a truth more meaningful because it is not delayed.

Christ's Church is committed to the communication of truth, and the Body of Christ, which is the Church, can only be built up—truly edified—by the quick and complete transmission of truth. Yet, while no truth is irrelevant, some truth is indispensable—especially that truth which helps us to appreciate our destiny more fully, and to pursue it more faithfully.

Speaking to journalists earlier this year on the feast of St. Francis de Sales, the patron of journalists, Pope Paul stated: "May you make known the real face of the Church, and work in unison with us for the great causes of mankind, especially for peace."

Surely, such an invitation is also a benediction, for if Sacred Scripture calls down a blessing on the feet of those messengers who bring the good news, we may call down a blessing not only on the modern messengers of the good news of timeless truth, but also on their modern instruments of timely transmission — instruments which make possible effective work in unison for the great causes of man and of God.

Demanding an End to Death-by-Abortion

Letter to the Faithful of the Archdiocese of Philadelphia, read at all Masses on January 20, 1974.

One year has passed since the United States Supreme Court issued the infamous abortion decision which prevents the states from protecting the inalienable right to life of unborn infants. The decision was greeted with incredible outrage and severe criticism. The Court was criticized for ignoring the scientific evidence that the human fetus is surely, from the earliest stages of its development, a human being. The Court denied the self-evident truth, proclaimed in the Declaration of Independence, that all men "are endowed by their Creator with certain inalienable rights," principal among which is the right to life itself. If this right is denied or subordinated to any other consideration, then no right is secure. The Court's decision contradicts the teaching of the Bible, and the deep religious convictions of millions of Americans, that human life—at every stage of its existence—is sacred and inviolable.

God's commandment, "You shall not kill," is honored by Americans of various religious affiliations, and by many who are not affiliated with a particular sect. God-fearing and God-loving people believe that no court, no legislative body, and no individual can arbitrarily deprive any innocent human being of the right to life. No right, over one's body or to privacy, can be exercised at the expense of the right to life of another human being. The Court clearly exceeded its competence in declaring that an unborn child is not a human person, and hence does not enjoy the protection of law. The existence of human life in the womb is a fact to be acknowledged. No human authority can deny personhood to human life. Whenever a conflict arises between the law of God and human authority, we must follow God's law.

Scholars who have studied the Supreme Court's abortion decision advise that the only practical way to provide for the legal protection of the right to life is to amend the Constitution of the United States. This course of action is difficult and complicated, but the protection of human life is so critical that it must be undertaken.

The amendment must clearly provide that every living unborn child enjoys the full protection of the law, and that no one's right to privacy, or to anything else, can supersede the basic right to life. In any civilized society, the protection of individual human rights is the primary responsibility of law. It is thus a matter of civic responsibility that all who affirm the sanctity of unborn human life pray, work, and strive to convince their fellow citizens of every and even no religious persuasion that unborn human life must enjoy equal protection of the law. We must also take practical action to express our commitment to life, and our opposition to death by abortion.

The following points constitute our Pro-Life Affirmation:

1. Abortion is a serious violation of God's law. Those who obtain an abortion, those who persuade others to have an abortion, and those who perform abortion procedures are guilty of breaking God's law. Our Church law has always attached serious penalties to this crime of abortion. That abortion is a shameful crime was reaffirmed by the Second Vatican Council: "God, the Lord of life, has entrusted to men the noble mission of safeguarding life, and men must carry it out in a manner worthy of them. Life must be protected with the utmost care from the moment of conception: abortion and infanticide are abominable crimes" (Pastoral Constitution on the Church in the Modern World, no. 27).

2. Serious problems do exist in connection with some pregnancies—problems such as illegitimacy, great emotional stress, possible disadvantages for the child after birth. But sound morality and sound law do not permit the solution of problems by the murder of human beings. Furthermore, allowing the taking of life in such circumstances introduces into society an insidious principle, which threatens the lives of many other innocent persons—the aged, the incurably ill, the retarded, the handicapped, and all who at some point may come to be regarded by society as undesirable or burdensome.

3. Charity and justice demand that we find ways to solve those problems which lead some women to consider abortion. In our diocese for many, many years now, we have made provisions to help women pregnant out of wedlock and their children. We shall continue to provide such services, and to do what we can to provide counsel and help to other women facing difficult pregnancy. At the same time, we take encouragement from the scientific advances of recent decades which have provided ways to support and maintain the life and health of the mother and the well-being of the child in the womb.

4. The Catholic Church is directing her educational and informational resources to a continuing pro-life program. This will include the scientific information on the humanity of the child and the child's developmental process; the moral responsibility and necessity for society to safeguard the life of the child at every stage of existence; the problems that may exist during pregnancy; and the humane and morally acceptable solutions to these problems which are available.

5. It is essential that our society adopt a positive attitude toward life, and reaffirm its commitment to the protection of life. Society has a duty to give encouragement, understanding, and support to women who experience difficult pregnancies, to intensify scientific investigation into the causes and cures of maternal disease and fetal abnormalities.

6. A constitutional amendment to protect the life of the unborn child is essential and urgently

needed. Congress should conduct hearings and move speedily to pass a pro-life amendment to the Constitution. Even then, concerted and continuous efforts will be needed to make sure that a majority of the American people are convinced that such an amendment is an absolute necessity. We appeal to the legislatures of the fifty states to memorialize Congress on behalf of a pro-life amendment. Well-planned and coordinated effort by citizens at the national, state, and local levels is of crucial importance. Our system of government requires citizen participation, and in this case there is a moral imperative of the highest order for the participation of all responsible citizens.

We call upon you and our fellow citizens to reject these decisions of our Supreme Court, and to demand an end to the wholesale slaughter of innocent unborn children that has followed them. We must and we will remove this blot on our national life.

Rededicating Ourselves to Protecting Life

Comments at the Pro-Life Demonstration at Independence Hall Federal Court House, on January 22, 1974.

It is a great privilege for me to be here today with so many thousands of you to rededicate ourselves to the principles on which our country was founded on this very place one hundred and ninety-eight years ago. This place is revered around the world as a cradle of liberty, because here our country's fathers proclaimed that all men were endowed by their Creator with certain inalienable rights.

Our founders recognized that these rights did not come from a particular religious belief—not Protestant, not Jewish, not Catholic—but from the God-given nature of man. These rights are human rights, they are God-given rights, and no government or group may deny them to any class of people. Our founders declared that the duty of government was not to deny human rights, but to protect them.

It is true that we have not reached the goals of our founders. Liberty and the pursuit of happiness have been denied for short periods and for long to many of our fellow Americans. But never until one year ago today was the inalienable right to life denied. Incredibly, this was denied to the most defenseless of God's creatures—the unborn.

Generations of Americans have worked and fought to make the freedoms guaranteed in our Declaration of Independence a reality. Let history record that we are continuing the fight in this year, 1974, and if need be in the coming years to safeguard the rights of all human beings, especially the unborn child. Let history also record that today we are rededicating ourselves to the proposition: "We hold these truths to be self-evident, that all men are created equal, that they are endowed by their Creator with certain inalienable rights, that among these are life, liberty, and the pursuit of happiness."

An awesome challenge faces every one of us to reverse the infamous decision of our Supreme Court, and to restore once and for all the God-given right to life.

May God strengthen our convictions; may God bless you and your work. He creates life. May He grant us the courage to protect it!

Morality, Law and War in a Nuclear Age

Address at the International Laws and Warfare Symposium, on June 19-20, 1974.

It is my pleasant duty as President of the United States Catholic Conference to welcome the members of the International Law Symposium to this inaugural meeting. I extend this welcome on behalf of the Conference, and especially on behalf of the bishops who funded this enterprise, some of whom are with us tonight.

I do not attempt to offer an analysis of the very complex and comprehensive agenda of issues which you will study. I merely wish to indicate the intent of the Catholic Conference in sponsoring this interdisciplinary analysis of the laws of warfare in light of the Christian moral tradition on the use of force.

My theme is that the endeavor we inaugurate tonight emerges from the convergence of several distinct elements, all of which point toward the need for an in-depth study of morality and modern war.

Over two decades ago the Italian theologian, Romano Guardini, formulated in general terms the structure of the moral question which this study will seek to articulate in a more specific, technical and precise manner. Guardini asserted that the basic question of the post-modern age is whether we can develop the moral capacity to control the power we have created. The logic of this formulation emphasizes the fact that in this post-modern era we can expand and develop our many forms of power faster than we can create moral limits to control power.

In the post-modern age, power is a multi-dimensional reality; it assumes scientific, technological, economic, political and strategic forms. Guardini's moral question, however, has special relevance to the paradox of nuclear power. Churchill had defined the paradox as a situation in which "safety will be the sturdy child of terror and survival the twin brother of annihilation."

The nuclear paradox remains with us today; only its scale has increased, and that to staggering dimensions in terms of economic costs and destructive capacity. We have lived almost a generation with "the delicate balance of terror"; while serious observers still debate whether it is growing more or less delicate, no one denies that it is ravaging billions of dollars of scarce resources simply to keep the terrifying balance. The superpowers alone now spend an estimated two hundred billion dollars for defense. Three years ago, while addressing the topic of injustice of the arms race at the Synod of Bishops in Rome, I sought to raise the general moral issue in these words:

"The Church should be relentless in its efforts to shape public opinion and to create a climate in which theology, and not technology, would give direction to the course of human events. Then men would understand why arms limitation is a necessary step to general disarmament, which is a prerequisite to international justice, in which men, convinced that the arms race is a treacherous trap and war a tragic folly, would direct their efforts and resources toward removing the cause of war—injustice."

Today, when Guardini's question still remains unanswered, when it is not yet clear whether we have both the moral wisdom and the political will to control the potential for destruction which we possess, I can only repeat my earlier remarks with even greater urgency.

While an exhortation to analysis and action on such an overwhelming issue is necessary, it is not sufficient. More than urgent exhortation is needed. To confront the ethical question we have to move to the empirical order of the political and strategic facts.

Moral argument—instrument of criticism and source of wisdom

While it is your function as trained specialists to identify all the factors of the empirical order of politics and strategy, I venture to indicate two broad aspects of the empirical question which have served as motivating causes for convoking this symposium. One aspect concerns what we are seeking to prevent happening; the other aspect is the result of what has happened to us, and through us, in the past decade.

Three decades into the nuclear age, our minimum necessary goal must still be to prevent the ultimate weapon from ever being used again. Statesmen, analysts and plain people all acknowledge that no rational political purpose could ever be served by breaking the nuclear barrier. Yet, we continue not only to produce our weapons, but to expand their size and destructive power. The dynamism at work is the logic of deterrence, but this logic has its moral and political limits. These limits are constantly being tested by rapid technological change and continuing strategic adaptation. Even as we gather to study the moral limits of the use of force, a new debate on strategic policy has been stimulated by Secretary Schlesinger's proposal for reshaping the strategic force structure. Indeed, on both sides of the current debate, moral warrants are introduced as reasons for supporting or opposing a new strategic position.

It is indeed a welcome development to have moral reasoning introduced into a political debate of such significance. In the face of such a development, however, we in the Church need to ask about the quality of moral discourse employed in the debate. Precisely used, moral argument can clarify, test and guide policy discussion; it can function as both an instrument of criticism and a source of wisdom. Misused, moral argument can be subordinated to political ends so that it serves simply to support decisions made on the basis of other factors. It is my hope and that of the Catholic Conference that the work of this symposium may help to assure a disciplined use of moral discourse in the current debate on strategic policy.

The Vietnam experience

A second dimension of empirical or strategic order which has moved us to convene this study is the Vietnam experience of the last decade. While the most devastating strategic consequences and moral damage of the war descended upon the Indochina peninsula, the impact of the brutal and tragic conflict upon us as a nation cannot be easily calculated. Even as the war continues to rage, the domestic implications of the conflict remain unanalyzed. We can identify the visible victims rather quickly: veterans whose medical, financial and social needs are not adequately met; exiles and conscientious objectors who languish in prison or a foreign land because demands of conscience placed them in opposition to a debated and debatable war; inhabitants of North and South Vietnam, Cambodia and Laos, whose land and lives must somehow be restored. Although we are far from consensus as a people, we have begun to debate the needs of these visible victims: policies and programs of assistance to the veterans; some form of amnesty for the exiled; forms of aid and assistance to former allies and adversaries.

These are not simple issues. But an even more difficult issue is to probe the moral questions which emerged from this form of "unconventional" warfare. The questions arose not only from the reasons for which the war was pursued, but most especially from the way in which it was fought. The massive numbers of civilian casualties, the nature and consequences of antipersonnel weapons, the drive toward totally mechanized warfare culminating in the bombing campaign of 1972—all raise the sharpest moral questions. The questions touch the principle of proportionality, the protection of civilian life, and the political purpose for which force can be used. These questions should not remain unanswered in the national psyche. Our purpose is not to have the symposium deal principally with Vietnam, but to analyze the kinds of moral issues which unconventional warfare poses.

Search for peace in the nuclear age

These diverse events and developments in the political and strategic orders have provoked within the Church a process of theological reflection about the stance of the Church in the face of modern warfare. Pius XII laid the foundation of this reflection in his Christmas Addresses. John XXIII, building upon the teaching of these addresses, elaborated in *Pacem in Terris* the striking vision of the problems and possibilities entailed in the search for peace in the nuclear age. It is hard to overestimate the impact this document has had on the Church's understanding of war and peace.

Finally, in Vatican Council II, this ecclesiological reflection on peace was taken a step further in The Pastoral Constitution on the Church in the Modern World. In this document, the Council Fathers tell us that "the whole human family faces an hour of supreme crisis in its advance toward maturity." Then they make the following response to this crisis:

"All these considerations compel us to undertake an evaluation of war with an entirely new attitude. The men of our time must realize that they will have to give a somber reckoning of their deeds of war, for the course of the future will depend greatly on the decisions they make today" (no. 80).

Two points about this powerful passage strike me as significant for our considerations. First, in a sense, the Council Fathers gave the whole Church a mandate through this paragraph to make the consideration of modern war a priority in the work of the Church. While the mandate undoubtedly applies to the universal Church, it unquestionably has special significance for the Church in the United States. Living in one of the global superpowers, the mandate weighs upon us heavily. Living in a democratic society where the Church has the possibility to address these questions in the political process, the mandate becomes our imperative to speak intelligently, passionately and prophetically for the cause of peace against the forces of war.

Secondly, although the mandate of the Council is clear, it is a mandate without a method. The Council Fathers in this passage stated the imperative of the moment — to evaluate war with a new attitude; they did not indicate what steps should be involved in this evaluation. They were calling for a work of theological, ethical and political development in the thinking of the Church. Quite properly, they left that work of development to those trained in the fields of theology, ethics, social science and law. It is to respond to this call that we have convoked this symposium. As bishops in the Catholic community, we respect your various competencies, and ask you to join with us in fulfilling the mandate of Vatican II by providing a method, a way of bringing the resources of the Christian tradition into creative tension and dialogue with facts of international relations today.

It is our hope and prayer that the fruits of your work will contribute to the pastoral life of the Christian community, and to the debate within the policy community about how we all can evaluate war with a new attitude, thereby contributing to peace on earth and to the development of peoples.

A Work on Behalf of All People

Address at the Annual Meeting Dinner of the Pennsylvania Catholic Conference on August 6, 1974.

The Pennsylvania Catholic Conference, as the bylaws declare, is established to give witness to spiritual values in public affairs, and to provide an agency for corporate Catholic service to the statewide community. All of the PCC efforts must be related and subordinated to the ultimate goal of promoting God's kingdom.

It is not a rare human trait to overlook the obvious. This trait enables so-called magicians to entertain audiences by tricks of illusion and "sleight of hand." This same trait leads some to infer that the PCC is a mere political and lobbying agency, and as such, is an unwarranted intrusion of the Church into the affairs of State. Because of this trait to overlook the obvious, it is at times useful and even necessary to recall the nature and purpose of the PCC.

The ecclesiastical and civil powers

When in reply to His questioners, our Lord said: "Then give to Caesar what is Caesar's, but give to God what is God's" (Mt. 22:21), He set forth the principle and the basis for the correlation of the two distinct and mutually independent powers—each supreme in its own province, and each subject to the Almighty—the Church and State.

Throughout the ages, the Church has taught that God has entrusted the charge of the human race to *two powers: ecclesiastical,* which has competence over the spiritual and supernatural interests of man; and the *civil,* which has competence over the temporal interests of men. Since each has power over the same subjects, God, the Author of both powers, chartered a course of correlation of both powers.

God Himself, through His divine Son, Jesus Christ, established the Church as a perfect and visible society. The Church is chartered by divine right as a visible, but spiritual and supernatural society because of the end for which it was founded, and because of the means used to achieve that end. It carries on its divine mission—guiding men to holiness and heaven—without interference and without hindrance. Since God is the Author of both powers, there should be no incompatibility or conflict between the ecclesial and civil power. Should such a conflict arise, then, because of the primacy of the spiritual over the material, and of the immortal over the mortal, the Church after the example of St. Peter must say: "Better for us to obey God than men" (Acts 5:29).

The ruling authority

It has been the constant teaching of the Church that every civilized community must have a ruling authority, striving for the common good. This authority, no less than society itself, has its source in nature, and consequently has God for its author. Civil authority is conferred by God not by an act of direct divine intervention, but as a necessary consequence of the nature and destiny of human beings. They cannot live rightly and reasonably without civil society, and civil society cannot function effectively without a governing authority. This authority is sanctioned and ratified by the Creator and Governor of the human race.

It is in this sense that St. Paul instructed the Romans: "Let everyone obey the authorities that are over him, for there is no authority except from God, and all authority that exists is established by God. As a consequence, the man who opposes authority rebels against the ordinance of God" (Rom. 13:1).

A false concept of civil power

The concept of the sovereignty of the people, i.e., that all civil power and authority resides in and derives from the people, without any reference to God, is a flattering one, but totally lacks any proof. All men are essentially alike and equal in their human dignity. Each man is his own master and has control of his life, and in no sense is under the rule of another individual or group of individuals. Such a concept of civil power contradicts the reality of inalienable rights, which the State must respect and protect. Such a theory of government could be used to justify the worst of Nazi atrocities. Man separated from God becomes inhuman to himself and to those of his kind, because the orderly relation of society presupposes the orderly relation of one's conscience with God — the source of truth, justice and love.

It has often been said that we the people of this country are a religious people, whose institutions presuppose a Supreme Being. Because they presuppose a Supreme Being, the people cannot claim to be themselves supreme; nor can they recognize anyone else's claim to be supreme. In a nation under God, no one can claim to be God; no one can arrogate to himself the powers of God; no one can presume to act as God.

While few men would be foolish enough to claim to be God, or to have His powers, there are many who compartmentalize their private and public life, and divorce their religious life from their political, social, and professional activities. Vatican Council II in the Pastoral Constitution on the Church in the Modern World said: "This split between the faith which many profess and their daily lives deserves to be counted among the more serious errors of our age" (no. 43). How often have we heard the stereotyped protest not to "impose" our brand of morality on others? There is no question of right or wrong — it is assumed to be wrong if it is somehow related to religion and morality.

Inscribing the divine law in the earthly city

The Council Fathers explained that Christ gave His Church no proper mission in the political, economic, or social order. The purpose He set before her is a religious one. "But out of this religious mission itself comes a function, a light, an energy which can serve to structure and consolidate the human community according to the divine law. As a matter of fact, when circumstances of time and place create the need, she can and indeed should initiate activities on behalf of all men" (Pastoral Constitution on the Church in the Modern World, no. 42).

In accord with the divine plan and will, all human activity should harmonize with the genuine good of the human race, and enable all men as individuals and as members of society to pursue their total vocation in time and in eternity.

The Council Fathers declared: "Laymen should also know that it is generally the function of their well-formed Christian conscience to see that the divine law is inscribed in the life of the earthly city.... The Christian who neglects his temporal duties neglects his duties towards his neighbor and even God, and jeopardizes his eternal salvation.... In the exercise of all their earthly activities, they can thereby gather their human, domestic, professional, social, and technical enterprises into one vital synthesis with religious values, under whose supreme direction all things are harmonized unto God's glory" (*Ibid.*, no. 43).

Though it may seem paradoxical, the Church as a visible society has a spiritual mission, and does not engage in purely political activity. Her role is to teach first her faithful children, and all who are disposed to listen to the Gospel truths. She does this by teaching and exhortation, and also with a view to penetrating and permeating all private and public life with the divine law. However, the Church's political aloofness does not entail inaction and disengagement on the part of citizens who are laity, faithful to ecclesial life; in particular, it does not mean failure to participate in the life of the nation.

Moreover, while the Church normally expresses herself in positive terms of teaching and exhortation, occasions may arise when the Church must resort to healthy criticism to denounce injustice courageously, with charity.

Even before the conciliar doctrine on the correlation of Church and State was written, the bishops of Pennsylvania carried out their primary responsibility as teachers in their respective dioceses, and they continue that responsibility of their office. Moreover, the bishops organized what is now the Pennsylvania Catholic Conference as an instrument through which citizens who are laity, faithful to ecclesial life, could make their presence felt at the State Legislative levels.

The work of the PCC, in which we are all engaged, is a work of the People of God. It is an instrument in which bishops manifest leadership and initiate activities on behalf of all men, with the single purpose of injecting into our society the tenets of divine law and will, so that all human life and activity would be harmonized unto God's glory.

For your valuable efforts to advance the work of the PCC, and through it to promote the kingdom of God, the bishops are deeply grateful. It is our prayer that in all PCC efforts we seek not vain human domination of public life, but rather the conformity of all human life and activity to God's will.

Deep Concern for the Lives of the Unborn

Statement on the vote of the State Legislature to override the Shapp Veto of Abortion Bill 1318, on September 11, 1974.

I congratulate our state Senators and Representatives on enacting into law, over the veto of Governor Shapp, a bill which will afford as much protection as is now constitutionally possible to the lives of unborn infants, and to the rights of fathers and families in the Commonwealth of Pennsylvania.

By once again giving their stamp of approval to Senate Bill 1318, the members of the General Assembly have made a substantial move toward fulfilling their obligation to guarantee protection for all human life, and to foster those values of family responsibility so essential to our society.

In taking their courageous action, our legislators not only showed their deep concern for the lives of the unborn, but also their concurrence with the efforts of citizens throughout the Commonwealth who sacrificed so much that those without voices would not become those without rights.

As I have said before, this is not an ideal law. An ideal solution would afford protection to all unborn children in this nation at all stages of their development, but this ideal can now be reached only by a constitutional amendment which requires action by our national congress and by three-fourths of our states. However, we believe that this law will save many unborn human lives—lives which would have been destroyed unless our citizens and our lawmakers had shown such a concern for the right to life which all of us so deeply treasure.

While we are grateful for the passage of this law, we must not diminish our efforts to work for further guarantees of the right to life through an appropriate constitutional amendment, and to show our abiding respect for all human life through the works of charity and mercy which are the responsibility not only of the Church, but of our entire society.

Human Rights and Reconciliation

Statement of the Synod—1974, presented by John Cardinal Krol, on October 23, 1974.

The Holy Father, in union with the bishops assembled at the Synod for the study of evangelization, issues the following message:

Two anniversaries of special significance to the Church and the world have occurred since the Synod of 1971: the tenth anniversary of Pope John's encyclical, *Pacem in Terris* (1963), and the twenty-fifth anniversary of the United Nations Declaration of Human Rights (1948). Both documents remind us that human dignity requires the defense and promotion of human rights.

We are gathered in a Synod whose theme is evangelization—the proclamation of the Good News of Jesus. While the truths about human dignity and rights are accessible to all, it is in the Gospel that we find their fullest expression and our stongest motive for commitment to their preservation and promotion. The relationship between this commitment and the ministry of the Church has been manifested in this Synod in our sharing of pastoral experiences, which reflect the transnational character of the Church, her entrance into the very consciences of people, and her participation in their suffering when rights are denied or violated.

Reflecting on these experiences in the light of the Gospel, we address this message on human rights and reconciliation to the Church and the entire world, especially to all in positions of responsibility. It is our desire to raise our voices on behalf of the voiceless victims of injustice.

Human dignity is rooted in the image and reflection of God in each of us. It is this which makes all persons essentially equal. The integral development of persons makes more clear the divine image in them. In our time the Church has grown more deeply aware of this truth; hence she believes firmly that the promotion of human rights is required by the Gospel, and is central to her ministry.

The Church desires to be more fully converted to the Lord and to perform her ministry by manifesting respect and regard for human rights in her own life. There is renewed consciousness in the Church of the role of justice in her ministry. The progress already made encourages us to continue efforts to conform ever more fully to the will of the Lord.

From her own experience, the Church knows that her ministry of fostering human rights in the world requires continued scrutiny and purification of her own life, her laws, institutions, and policies. The Synod of 1971 declared that "anyone who ventures to speak to people about justice must first be just in their eyes." Awareness of our limitations, faults and failures in justice helps us to understand better the failings of other institutions and individuals. In the Church, as in other institutions and groups, purification is needed in internal practices and procedures, and in relationships with social structures and systems whose violations of human rights deserve censure.

No nation today is faultless where human rights are concerned. It is not the role of the Synod to identify specific violations; this can better be done at the local level. At the same time we desire by our words and actions to encourage those who work for human rights, to call upon those in authority to promote human rights, and to give hope to those who suffer violations of their rights. We call attention here to certain rights most threatened today.

The right to life: This right is basic and inalienable. It is grievously violated in our day by abortion and euthanasia, by widespread torture, by acts of violence against innocent parties, and by the scourge of war. The arms race is an insanity which burdens the world and creates the conditions for even more massive destruction of life.

The right to eat: This right is directly linked to the right to life. Millions today face starvation. The nations and peoples of the world must make a concerted act of solidarity in the forthcoming United Nations Food Conference. We call upon governments to undergo a conversion in their attitude toward the victims of hunger; to respond to the imperatives of justice and reconciliation;

and speedily to find the means of feeding those who are without food.

Socio-economic rights: Reconciliation is rooted in justice. Massive disparities of power and wealth in the world, and often within nations, are a grave obstacle to reconciliation. Concentration of economic power in the hands of a few nations and multi-national groups, structural imbalances in trade relations and commodity prices, failure to balance economic growth with adequate distribution both nationally and internationally, widespread unemployment and discriminatory employment practices, as well as patterns of global consumption of resources all require reform if reconciliation is to be possible.

Politico-cultural rights: Reconciliation in society and the rights of the person require that individuals have an effective role in shaping their own destinies. They have a right to participate in the political process freely and responsibly. They have a right to free access to information, freedom of speech and press, as well as freedom of dissent. They have a right to be educated, and to determine the education of their children. Individuals and groups must be secure from arrest, torture and imprisonment for political or ideological reasons, and all in society, including migrant workers, must be guaranteed juridical protection of their personal, social, cultural and political rights. We condemn the denial or abridgment of rights because of race. We advocate that nations and contesting groups seek reconciliation by halting persecution of others and by granting amnesty, marked by mercy and equity, to political prisoners and exiles.

The right of religious liberty: This right uniquely reflects the dignity of the person as this is known from the Word of God and from reason itself. Today it is denied or restricted by diverse political systems in ways which impede worship, religious education and social ministry. We call upon all governments to acknowledge the right of religious liberty in words and to foster it in deeds, to eliminate any type of discrimination, and to accord to all, regardless of their religious convictions, the full rights and opportunities of citizens.

We reassert that the Church must strive to be a sign and source of reconciliation among all peoples. People have a right to hope; the Church today should be a sign and source of hope. Hence the Church offers pardon to all who have persecuted or defamed her, and pledges openness and sympathetic understanding to all who question, challenge and confront her. We call finally upon each person to recognize the responsibility which he or she has in conscience for the rights of others. Enlightened in our understanding of evangelization, and strengthened in our commitment to proclaim the Good News, we affirm our determination to foster human rights and reconciliation everywhere in the Church and in the world today.

His Holiness, Pope Paul VI's comment on the document on Human Rights

To the faithful in St. Peter's Square on October 27, 1974.

The Bishops' Synod closed yesterday. It seems to us that it has assumed the significance of an historic moment, and of orientation for the Church in the fact and aim of rediscovering and reaffirming her mission in the world. This mission is to announce Christ, to make Him live in hearts through the power of the Spirit, and thus to promote the transfiguration of mankind (cf. L. Bouyer, "L'Eglise," 572). Nothing new here, except the novelty of grasping once again this religious-social innovation of life and of history. This is the Gospel. This is the Council. And we experienced in the Synod a secret energy, derived precisely from the Gospel, and working with a new and youthful imperative in our times—and may God will it also for future generations. It is a conclusion, and it is a beginning. The Synod may perhaps qualify as an historic event—which fact made it difficult to include in an improvised final document the overflowing richness of its contents.

However, almost bursting forth from the fullness of synodal meditation was a message. And you are aware of it. It is even understandable to those who are not used to theological reflection, but who are open to and enthused about its human and sociological consequences.

We are referring to the appeal regarding "Human Rights," read by Cardinal Krol on Wednesday the 23rd, in the twenty-first general assembly of the Synod and unanimously approved by the Synod Fathers.

It is beautiful. Once again we see that the affirmation of the rights of God generates the affirmation of the rights of man. This is the religion of the Gospel: the love of God is the root of love of neighbor—and everyone in the world is our neighbor! The renewed affirmation of the human and sociological value and duty of theological and consequential rights of man comes at an appropriate moment today when there is so much talk of mankind's liberation and advancement towards hard-to-reach levels of justice, equality, fraternity and solidarity. Human dignity is thus re-vindicated in virtue of that religious sentiment which many try to render senseless, and at the very moment when civil society, attaining the zenith of its happy and progressive evolution, still tolerates contradictory conditions and theories, and runs the risk of new and frightful conflagrations.

History is always a drama of obscure destinies. And the Church, dauntless and loving, raises her banner of justice and peace.

Let us give thanks to the Lord, and renew our commitment to serve and love every man, our brother.

The Food Crisis

At the Symposium on "Hunger and the American Conscience," on February 11, 1975.

Crisis of civilization and of solidarity

Pope Paul VI called the food crisis a crisis of civilization and solidarity. Of civilization because it involves the most fundamental human and spiritual values. Of solidarity because of the imbalance between individuals, which results from the insufficient willingness to contribute to a better distribution of available resources.

The causes of the crisis are many and varied. The prime responsibility must be placed on a predatory egoism reflected in an overriding pursuit of wealth, profit, and power, even at the cost of impoverishing entire continents, and despoiling them of their natural resources. The antidote for such egoism is a sense of human solidarity and brotherhood, and a determination to provide short-term emergency relief and long-term programs geared to promoting the self-sufficiency of all people.

Dimensions of the crisis

United Nations food experts say that 32 nations are hard pressed to buy grain, fertilizer and petroleum needed desperately to stave off the starvation of 700 million out of a total population of 900 million.

Some experts assert that unless more aid comes quickly, at least two million people literally will starve to death in less than a year, and added millions will die of diseases related to malnutrition. Still others will suffer mental and physical damage from an inadequate diet.

Areas of chronic famine

1. India, Bangladesh, Pakistan, Sri-Lanka: 726 million people.

2. Sub-Saharan Africa, including Ethiopia, Mauritania, Chad, Niger, Upper Volta and Mali: 65 million people.

It is estimated that 5 to 10 million people are affected in the belt that stretches across Africa for thousands of miles at the southern extremity of the Sahara desert because of the encroaching arid sands of the Sahara. In 1973 the desert advanced 60 miles into the Sahel (shore), forcing a mass migration of people southward. Some climatologists fear that this crisis is but the initial stage of a thirty-year period of diminishing rainfall.

3. Laos and Cambodia: 10.8 million people.

4. Latin America—Haiti, El Salvador, Honduras, Guiana: 12.7 million people.

Shrinking grain reserves

The world grain supply dropped to the lowest level in more than two decades from a 95- to a

22-day supply. Between 1972 and 1973 grain stocks of exporting countries plunged from 49 to 29 million tons.

Food reserves dropped from 25% in 1970 to 11% in 1973. This caused an increase in prices so that from 1971 to 1974 the price of grain jumped from $62 to $169; rice from $1.29 to $5.17; and soy beans from $1.26 to $2.27.

The situation is aggravated by the quadrupling of petroleum prices. This caused developing nations to divert more of their meager resources to petroleum and less to agricultural production. At the same time, this increase was accompanied by a drop in the products normally produced by the developing countries, such as rubber, coffee, cotton and tin.

Since 1955, under the Food for Peace Plan, the United States has supplied wheat, rice and other commodities free, or at bargain prices, at a cost to American taxpayers of $23 billion.

The United States and the food crisis

A deep sense of grievance has developed against the United States in the developing world because of the drop in food aid. There has indeed been a drop. The Food for Peace Plan shipments started with 3.3 million metric tons in 1955, rose above 18 million tons in 1962 to 1966, but dropped to 10 million tons in 1972, and to 3.2 million tons in 1974.

There is criticism that the United States uses food aid as a means of advancing its own goals. Thus the Federal Pl 480 program in 1974 gave South Vietnam seven times the assistance given to Bangladesh, and Cambodia received twelve times the aid requested for the nations in the Sub-Sahara (Sahel) area in Africa.

There is criticism that the food aid is a means of economic gain for the United States. Actually, five corporations in the United States control 90% of the world's grain reserves. Four of these corporations are privately owned, and these are not required by law to give an accounting to the Federal Government of their operations.

The United States is also criticized because it is one of the number of countries which comprise 30% of the world's population, but consumes over 51% of the grain produced in the world. In Canada and the United States, the annual per capita consumption of grain is about 800 kgs (1,760 lbs.) of which only 90 kgs (198 lbs.) are used directly by humans and the rest is used for cattle raising, using approximately 10 kgs of grain to produce one kg of meat. It takes 7 pounds of grain to produce one pound of beef; four of grain for one of pork, and three of grain for one of poultry. In 1974 a record poundage of beef was produced for a record per capita consumption of 116.5 pounds. Official predictions are that 8 to 10% more cattle will be slaughtered in 1975 than in 1974, which saw the record kill of 36.8 million head.

The United States is criticized because — at a time when food prices are spiraling, the international market is high, millions of people are faced with starvation, and many of them are literally starving to death—the U.S. Department of Agriculture has paid American farmers to hold crop land out of production. The U.S.D.A. Assistant Secretary and the executive assistant to the Secretary of Agriculture at first denied, but later issued a statement conceding error. (Cf. *Philadelphia Inquirer*, lead editorial on December 18, 1974). In their brief statement and press release, the two officials declared that for idling wheat, feed grain and cotton acreage, the U.S. Government had paid farmers $2.3 billion in 1973; $3.5 billion in 1972; and $2.8 billion in 1971. Such inhumane and economically absurd policies deserve criticism. It seems incredible that two such high officials could have made an oversight of the expenditure of $8.6 billion in the taxpayers' money.

The U.S. is also criticized because it is one of the leading nations which in 1973 spent $207 billion—or 6.7% of the gross national product of all the nations of the world—for armaments. This amount is 30 times the amount of aid given by developed nations to developing nations. Additionally, $20 billion was paid to 400,000 research scientists who seek to develop, refine and perfect instruments of destruction.

However, this criticism cannot be limited to developed nations, because all the Third World nations increased their percentage of the total amount spent by all the nations of the world for armaments from 5.2% in 1955 to 14.3% in 1973. In 1973, Latin America alone increased its spending for armaments by 23%. It appears that the hunger for armaments is more acute than the hunger for bread.

The criticism of the U.S. is not entirely without merit. No one can reasonably deny that in view of the mass starvation of millions, the U.S. should not decrease, but increase its food aid programs. At the same time, the criticism directed against the U.S. seems to ignore the past record of U.S. performance in foreign food aid.

The record shows that since the end of World War II, the U.S. has contributed about $197 billion in aid to some 140 nations — a sum equivalent to more than 40% of the current national debt. The fact is that the U.S. has been the world's largest and most generous donor of food to help the hungry and the dying. Over the last 8 years, the U.S. provided 84% of all food aid given by developed countries. The Secretary of Agriculture estimates that the U.S. has shipped about $25 billion in food aid in the last twenty years.

The foreign aid program hit its peak in years when the U.S. was prosperous, jobs were plentiful, living standards rising, prices holding fairly steady, and the country enjoyed a fat trade balance. None of that is true today. The gross national product is not climbing, as it did in the past. Prices of food have increased 36% in the past two years. There was an 11% rate of inflation in 1974, and the President's new budget lists an average inflation rate of 11.3% for this year. Unemployment has risen to 7.5 million or about 8.2% of the work force. Grain reserves are being depleted. Out of every dollar of income in the United States, 37 cents goes for taxes. The average workingman must work the first three hours of every day to earn the money he pays in taxes. Last year, the increase in taxes outstripped all other price increases in the consumers' budget, e.g., social security taxes increased 21.6%, personal income taxes increased 26.5%, whereas the cost of food increased about 12%, the cost of housing about 13.5%, and the cost of transportation about 14.3%.

Coupled with these serious internal problems is a measure of disenchantment on the part of a number of legislators, because some of the recipients of U.S. aid have, almost consistently, lined up against the U.S. in critical international situations. Several Latin American and African countries which have received aid have nationalized American businesses and have raised barriers to imports of U.S. goods. India, which time and again has been saved from famine by American food shipments, seldom misses a chance to denounce U.S. diplomatic and military action. As the outgoing U.S. Ambassador to India, Daniel Moynihan, said: "They don't know how to cultivate us. They go around and make up lists of what America has done wrong." At the same time India has found funds to develop the atom bomb.

The U.S. foreign aid program is being increasingly criticized and opposed even by once-friendly lawmakers. Some allege that in some instances U.S. aid has held back efforts by the developing countries to increase their own farm production.

Rankling under the quadrupled price of oil, they point out that in 1975 the U.S. contributed $28 million towards the $85 million budget of the United Nations relief agency for Palestine Refugees. Saudi Arabia, the world's leading oil exporter, and the professed champion of the Palestinians, contributed only $650,000.

Canada and the U.S. are two countries that have managed to produce a surplus of grain. At the World Conference of Food, Canada pledged a 20% increase in food aid to foreign nations, bringing the Canadian aid to a million tons of grain a year over the next three years. The U.S. was criticized for not making a similar commitment on the spot. A member of the Canadian delegation at the Food Conference commented: "We have always considered that the United States had done more than its share." The record shows that over the last 8 years, the U.S. provided 84% of all food aid given by developed countries. Even at its lowest level in 1974 the U.S. shipped 3.2 million tons. On February 3, President Ford announced a budget of $1.6 billion for the U.S. Food for Peace Program, which will increase food shipments to 5.5 million tons of grain.

It is easy to criticize, and beyond question some of our foreign aid policies deserve criticism. But it is better to know all the facts and to understand the circumstances which led to a decrease in our food aid programs. If we are to develop any kind of effective program for increasing aid, we must appreciate the concerns of our legislators, and the changing situations in our own country. Congressmen do ask what all the foreign aid does for their constituents—for the people back home. We must help them appreciate that the people back home will always respond "yes" to the question: "Shall we do all we can to keep people in the poor countries from starving?" We must convince them that the U.S. should not abandon its tradition of helping needy people, both at home and abroad.

The Church and the food crisis

1. The right to eat is an essential component of the right to life, and it is a basic human right which the Church must promote. This right is based on the fact that all the goods of the earth are destined primarily for universal use and for the subsistence of all men, before any individual appropriation.

2. To protect this right, the Church should support a restructuring of the food policy: increasing emergency aid, the establishment of an international grain reserve and technical assistance for other nations, with food seen as a sacred resource—as a trust to be shared and not a weapon to be used.

3. The Church must maintain the factual and moral dimensions of the food crisis as current news; support efforts to develop a strategy to control food prices for the consumer, and to have reasonable accountability from corporations that control the world's grain reserves.

4. The Church must continue to provide an example to the world, by its programs of relief to the needy. For over 30 years, the Catholics

of the United States, through the Bishops' Catholic Relief Services, have carried on a program of relief that averages over $150 million annually. Additionally, it develops special emergency programs in times of crisis. For example, with the bishops, priests, people, and governmental and private agencies, the Catholic Relief Services channelled a special program of relief to the African drought areas, which as of November 30, 1974, had a value of $6.8 million. As of the same date the Catholic Relief Services Africa Drought Fund had a balance of close to $2 million.

Our Lord, when faced with hungry crowds, commanded His disciples, "Give them something to eat." His compassion was accompanied by the effective action of the miraculous multiplication of loaves. The Church also must be compassionate, and must strive to promote effective action.

The possibility of a solution

In his address to the World Food Conference, Pope Paul said that the threat of hunger and the burden of malnutrition are not an inevitable destiny; that nature is not unfaithful to man, and that its productive capacity on land and in the seas remains immense and is still largely unexplored. He mentioned that it is generally acknowledged that 50% of the arable land in the world has not yet been cultivated.

There are those who seem to ignore the potentials of increasing food production and carry on a one-sided campaign against demographic growth. In his speech to the World Food Conference, Pope Paul VI said: "It is inadmissible that those who have control of the wealth and resources of mankind should try to resolve the problem of hunger by forbidding the poor to be born, or by leaving to die of hunger children whose parents do not fit into the framework of theoretical plans based on pure hypotheses about the future of mankind. In times gone by, in a past that we hope is now ended, nations resorted to war to seize their neighbors' riches. But is it not a new form of warfare to impose a restrictive demographic policy on nations to ensure that they will not claim their just share of the earth's goods?"

In a news conference on November 12th, a Methodist Churchman said that the issue of population control "should not be used as an excuse to avoid facing injustices in the economic and political spheres." In his address he said that Churches share in the blame "by their heretical maintenance of the status quo in spite of a dynamic faith which calls for radical change in attitudes and acts towards a more humane existence for all."

A long- and short-range solution to the food crisis demands confidence in God, who neglects none of His children, and confidence in man—made to the image and likeness of God—who is capable of making the resources of the universe yield their full potential.

We must not only recognize the rights of every man to the goods necessary for life, but must be ready to make the sacrifices necessary to place such goods at the disposal of every man. To this end courageous reforms aimed at eliminating the obstacles and the structural trade imbalance must be launched. Production must be increased and adequate means of distribution must be safeguarded.

Above all, we must overcome the type of egoism which is destructive of the sense of human solidarity and fraternity, and adopt a policy of sharing not only that which may be superfluous, but also that which is necessary to help our brothers avoid death by starvation.

On the Guilty Verdict Rendered in the Abortion-Related Case in Boston

Statement of February 15, 1975.

The guilty verdict in the abortion-related charge of manslaughter is not surprising. The issue was not one of abortion but of the destruction of human life following an abortion.

The verdict was made by peers who had no choice except to base their decision on the compelling evidence presented in the case. The jury is saying that a doctor has no right to kill an aborted fetus that is alive.

This case illustrates the full impact of the Supreme Court decision. The lack of respect for human life is not confined to the unborn child, but is being extended to the child after separation from its mother, even as it was extended in Japan following the legalization of abortion. Nothing short of a return to a total respect for human life, born and unborn, will eliminate abuse.

Some have expressed concern that the decision may inhibit abortions. We pray to God that it will and that at least some human lives may be saved.

We Must Live as a Family

At the Dinner Reception in his honor in Cairo, Holy Year, 1975.

Less than three weeks ago, I left Philadelphia as a spiritual director of the Holy Year Pilgrimage from the Archdiocese of Philadelphia. The Holy Year proclaimed by Pope Paul has as its theme Spiritual and Moral Renewal and Reconciliation of Man with God and of Man with His Neighbor.

The first lap of the Pilgrimage took place at the holy shrines in Rome; the second at the holy shrines of the Holy Land. We have continued through Jordan, Lebanon, and Egypt, not with any official mandate. We have an able representative of the United States government and an equally capable representative of the Holy See.

I come as a pilgrim, as one who is deeply interested in this theme of reconciliation. Our Lord Jesus Christ gave us a very simple formula: love God, love neighbor; do not render evil for evil.

Almost since the world began, not by any divine plan but through the weaknesses and failures of human beings, there have been problems and complications. Our age is no different than any of the others. We have them today.

We can no longer afford the luxury of divisions, of recriminations, of placing blame one upon the other. We must look to the reality that exists, the problems that exist, and recognize the fact that we are all children of the same Father; that we must live as a family; that there is no other successful plan for living in this world except to live as brothers, as children of the same Father.

I have come to Egypt at the invitation of a dear friend, congenial host, and a little bit of a "slave driver" as far as a tourist guide is concerned. He starts off in the morning, and he has thirty-three places to visit in the first hour and a half, and says that we do not have time off for a rest after the noonday meal because there are so many things to see.

I can never be sufficiently grateful to Cardinal Sidarouss for his cordiality and his efficiency as a tour guide. Likewise, Archbishop Glourieux has been my host—I've eaten at his table and for that I'm tremendously grateful to you, Your Excellency, and for this overwhelming reception I am equally grateful.

I have no pretense; I have no solutions. I have no formula other than that which our Lord provided. A simple formula, yet an unfailing one, and that is that we must—whatever the causes were in the past, whatever our differences were in the past—we must begin to eliminate animosity, hostility, recriminations, and begin to live as children of the same Father, as brothers.

I certainly hope that my visit to Egypt may have been the occasion to reflect at least my own sympathetic concern for human rights, for human dignity of all the people—not just some, but of all the people—and particularly the people of this great land that was made sacred by the Holy Family during their flight into Egypt.

For your cordiality, for your generosity, for the good will that I've seen, I am profoundly grateful.

The Need for a Rebirth of Discipline and Morality

Homily at St. Mary's Church, Philadelphia, on July 4, 1976, at the Bicentennial Liturgy of Thanksgiving and "Te Deum."

"May your kindness, O Lord, be upon us who have put our hope in you" (Ps. 33:22).

On this two hundredth anniversary of our nation's independence, we have assembled in this historic church to thank God for His many blessings upon our country and its people; to beg His mercy and forgiveness for our sins and failures, and to implore His guidance and providential care as we enter the third century of our national life.

St. Mary's and the Founding Fathers

This Church of St. Mary — the major part of which was built in 1763 — transcends the barrier of time and unites us with the Founding Fathers and with events connected with the founding of our nation. George Washington, Madison and the First Continental Congress attended Evening Prayer services in this church on October 9, 1774.

The Second Continental Congress attended services here on September 8, 1777, and with the President attended a *Te Deum* service for the Declaration of Independence on July 4, 1779. The same Congress attended a *Te Deum* service on November 4, 1781, for the victory over Cornwallis at Yorktown. Washington and the members of the Constitutional Convention attended Sunday Mass here on May 27, 1787. It is our privilege to participate in the Bicentennial thanksgiving service in the same edifice in which our Founding Fathers worshipped.

E Pluribus Unum — Catholic unity

It is our nation's boast that political unity has been achieved out of wide diversity — E Pluribus Unum. To be Catholic means to be united, but diverse. The participation of His Excellency, Archbishop Jadot, Apostolic Delegate, symbolized the unity of all Catholics — of every race, color, and culture — with the Vicar of Christ, His Holiness Pope Paul VI. The presence of the Holy Father's representative reflects the Gospel principle that we render to God the things that are God's and to Caesar — to country — the things that are Caesar's. Our fidelity to God and to country are not only compatible with, but are a requisite of our faith. Patriotism is a virtue. Our love of country is a love of preference, not of exclusion, because we must love all members of the human family.

Declaration of Independence a declaration of dependence on God

We commemorate today the Bicentennial of our nation—the Declaration of Independence. This Declaration has deep religious foundations, and enshrines forever in our history sound moral principles, religious convictions, and inalienable rights given by our Creator. It is in fact a declaration of dependence upon God. It articulates the principle that the spiritual is supreme; that man is of divine origin and possesses inalienable rights solely by reason of endowment by his Creator. These rights—to life, to liberty, and to the pursuit of happiness—have their foundation in God-given human dignity, and they must be respected and protected, and may not be violated or abrogated by the State.

Belief in God is the cornerstone of our American philosophy of government. The American concept of freedom is centered in God—not in man alone. Explicit in the American principle and practice has been the recognition of God as the origin of human existence and freedom, the ultimate authority in human life, and the destiny of human aspiration. Our Founding Fathers have told us that a nation must begin with God in theory, proceed with God's help in practice, be animated with religious conviction of God's active presence, or collapse when it abandons God in principle or in practice. Abraham Lincoln expressed this thought in the words: "I recognize the sublime truth...that those nations only are blest whose God is the Lord."

American and French Revolutions

It is well to recall today that there were two revolutions in the last quarter of the 18th century. Both were fiercely committed to the goal of securing and safeguarding human freedom. The leaders of the American Revolution centered the concept of freedom in God, and acknowledged God as the source of man's inalienable rights. The leaders of the French Revolution not only ignored God and failed to seek His guidance, but turned upon the Christian religion in angry denial. Churches were closed and Church leaders were forced to swear oaths to the State and the Revolution that were practical denials of God. The French Revolution inaugurated a reign of violence and terror. Thousands were carted through the streets to the guillotine. Robespierre, who led the people in worshipping false gods, was himself executed on the guillotine. The French Revolution, which was inspired in part by the revolution of the thirteen colonies, began in 1789, and by 1799 had not only failed, but had made it possible for France to fall into the hands of a despotic military adventurer, Napoleon Bonaparte.

Why did the French Revolution fail in ten years, and the effects of the American Revolution endure after two hundred years? The French experiment failed because its concept of liberty was wholly subjective — a total creation of the human will, detached from God and His laws. The American experiment acknowledged God as the source of man's inalienable rights. God is the cornerstone of our philosophy of government. Today, we do well to strengthen our conviction that if belief in God ceases to be a factor in our ideology and in our life, the national structure built thereon will eventually collapse.

We are a religious people

The framers of the Constitution appealed "to the Supreme Judge of the world for the rectitude of our intentions." They professed their firm reliance on the protection of divine Providence. Washington averred that religion and morality are the indispensable supports of our form of government. He cautioned that national morality cannot prevail to the exclusion of religious principles, and that education must be imbued with religion. When Lincoln in 1861 left Springfield for Washington, he told his friends, "Without the assistance of that Divine Being, who ever attended him (Washington), I cannot succeed. With that assistance, I cannot fail. Trusting Him, who can go with me and remain with you, and be everywhere for good, let us confidently hope that all will yet be well."

Our Supreme Court declared: "We are a religious people whose institutions presuppose a Supreme Being." Justice Steward observed: "The history of the religious tradition of our people is reflected in the countless practices of our institutions and officials of our government." The Great Seal of the United States, imprinted on the reverse side of every one dollar bill, has the inscription: "Annuit Coeptis Novus Ordo

Seclorum"—"God has favored our undertaking—a New Order of Ages." Our coinage carries the reminder that it is "In God We Trust." We pledge allegiance to our flag, and to the reality of "One Nation Under God."

America is great because America is good

The French historian of modern democracy, Alexis de Tocqueville, studied and wrote books about the American and French Revolutions. After his nine-month visit to the United States in 1831, he wrote:

"I sought for the greatness and genius of America in fertile fields and boundless forests: it was not there.

"I sought for it in her free schools and her institutions of learning: it was not there.

"I sought for it in her matchless Constitution and democratic Congress: it was not there.

"Not until I went to the Churches and Temples of America and found them aflame with righteousness did I understand the greatness of America.

"America is great because America is good. When America ceases to be good, America will cease to be great."

America's greatness is attributable not to our military power; not to our soaring gross national product; not to our high standards and quality of life; not to our natural resources and economic power. It is attributable to our righteousness; to our acknowledgement of God's existence, His moral law and His special Providence. It is attributable to our firm dependence upon God—to religion and morality, which are the indispensable supports of good government.

Lincoln, who acknowledged the sublime truth that only those nations are blest whose God is the Lord, lamented: "We have been the recipients of the choicest bounties of heaven; we have grown in numbers, wealth and power as no other nation has ever grown. But, we have forgotten God...."

Our country has been good, great and powerful. Yet, as much as we love our country, we must acknowledge that it is not God's kingdom on earth; it has its faults and failures. Our citizens and our government officials are not free of temptation, of sin, of injustice and corruption. But with all her faults and failures, we love our country and are proud of her positive accomplishments, just as we are ashamed of her failures. ures.

Corrective criticism

True love of country is compatible with intelligent corrective criticism of defects. Regrettably, we live in an age of captious, acrid and factional criticism. Such criticism gives comfort to our potential adversaries, and tends to destroy confidence in the ability of our people to govern themselves. We are a government of the people, by the people and for the people. Trenchant, corrective criticism is a dynamic of our form of government. Such criticism is, in fact, a form of self-criticism, since we as a people bear responsibility for our government. It is in this spirit of corrective criticism, without malice or hostility, and with charity for all, that we voice our concerns about certain trends which we consider detrimental to our nation.

Concerns about certain trends

We are concerned about the trend to minimize or ignore our heritage of dependence on the grace and strength of God. We are concerned about the tendency of the Supreme Court to interpret the Constitution by principles alien to the legal philosophy that gave it its existence. These alien principles cause the erosion of the very rights the Constitution intended to protect, and in their final impact betray our American heritage. We are concerned that in a nation in which over 95% of the people believe in God and over 60% of the people acknowledge membership in a Church, some of the Supreme Court decisions are based on a secularistic philosophy of life. This philosophy claims that God has no practical place in determining the rights of human beings, and alleges that a God-derived moral law is not the foundation of civil law as the Declaration of Independence asserted.

While we subscribe to the principle of separation of Church and State, we cannot subscribe to the interpretation which extends that separation to religion and to education. Individually and as a nation we must strive to restore the teaching of religious and moral principles, without which we cannot survive as a free people. To promote our common good and to insure a sound social order, the Supreme Court must be as decisive in denying tax funds for the teaching of sectarian dogma as it must be firm in encouraging the teaching of the basic religious and moral principles that are the indispensable supports of our form of government.

Millions of American parents are convinced that religion is an essential ingredient of education. They exercise their constitutional right and freedom to "control and direct the education of their children." They respect the Constitution and do not request, nor have they received, nor would they accept government funding for the teaching of religion. They know that teaching religion in Church-related schools does not change the essential nature, effectiveness and value of the secular subjects taught in such schools. They resent the practical exclusion from the benefits of educational taxes which they are forced to pay throughout their entire lifetime. They share the hope expressed by Chief Justice Burger that: "At some future date the Court will come to a more enlightened and tolerant view of the First Amendment's guarantee of free exercise of religion, thus eliminating the denial of equal protection of children in Church-sponsored schools, and take a more realistic view that carefully limited aid to children is not a step toward establishing a State religion."

We are concerned that the Supreme Court, by reading into the Constitution meanings its framers never intended it to have, have denied to students in public schools the "right to know" and to learn about God, the source of their inalienable rights. They have also denied to teachers and students in these schools the free exercise of religion. The freedom of religion may not be denied to any person or excluded from any place in this nation. By judicial "fiat" the freedom of religion has in fact been denied to teachers and students in the public schools.

We are gravely concerned that Justices of the Supreme Court have denied the most fundamental of all rights—the right to life—to children in their mothers' wombs. In a decision which ignored facts acknowledged by scientists, and contradicted sound principles of law and logic, the Supreme Court subordinated human life in the womb to the whims of individuals. While we subscribe to the principles of the right of privacy and the right of an individual over one's body, no right can be asserted over the right to life of another. No right can be exercised at the expense of the life of another human being. The Supreme Court's abortion decision is morally evil and must be reversed. What is morally wrong by the laws of God cannot be legally right by the decisions of a court.

We are even more concerned about the recent decision which ruled that states may not require parental consent in the case of an unmarried minor, or spousal consent in the case of a married woman, before an abortion can be performed. This decision gives abortion precedence over the right of husbands to participate fully in decisions affecting their marriage, and the right of parents to govern their children. This decision is an invitation to licentiousness. It is in fact the granting of a license to minors to be promiscuous, to commit fornication. There is no constitutional basis, as Justice White noted, for a "rule that the State must assign a greater value to a mother's decision to cut off a potential human life by abortion than to a father's decision to let it mature into a live child." This decision is a continuing aggression by the Court on the family structure.

We should be concerned about the social engineers whose demand for contraceptive population limitation has become a demand for abortion. Doctor Hellman, Deputy Assistant Secretary of the Department of Health, Education and Welfare, lamenting what he described as a faltering national will to face population issues, said: "No country has reduced its population growth significantly without resorting to abortion."

The grounds for depopulation is the alleged inability of the earth to provide food, minerals and energy for the increasing numbers. According to the tables of world mineral resources presented at the 1949 United Nations World Conference on Resources, we have already exhausted the entire world supplies of copper, lead, zinc, and some other materials. The fact is that the estimates were wrong. These materials have not been exhausted. Moreover, the predicted population increases have not been realized. Our potential for generating nuclear power has not been developed, and the energy reaching the earth from the sun is far in excess of any conceivable needs, once we develop the technology of harnessing it.

Prescinding from the serious moral aspects of the anti-life syndrome, we should be concerned about the adverse impact on our society. We are growing old, not only as a nation, but also as a people. At the turn of the century, one out of twenty-four persons was over sixty-five years of age. The ratio today is one out of ten, and at the present rate it will be one out of eight at the end of the century. Our Social Security program is now troubled. The anti-life programs are diminishing our most valuable resource—human beings—skilled workers. The Soviets, who encouraged population limitation, are now attacking it as a degraded form of imperialism designed to destroy the vitality of the peoples of developing countries. It is also significant that at the 1974 International Population Conference at Bucharest there was the remarkable alliance between China and the Vatican opposing the American proposals for world-wide population limitation.

Washington said that morality cannot be maintained without religion. It is a historical fact that great nations have died by suicide—through moral, social, cultural and economic decay. The elimination of religion from the public program of education is causing the religious and moral impoverishment of our nation. Between 1960 and 1970, while the population increased 13%, crimes increased 176%. The crime rate has tripled in the last 15 years. In 1973 the homicide rate of our ten largest cities was higher than that of

Northern Ireland. One of the cities with a population comparable to it had a homicide rate four times higher. Terrel H. Bell, United States Commissioner of Education, said: "We need a rebirth of both discipline and moral development in American education."

Jefferson said that "As government grows, freedom recedes." We should be deeply concerned about the explosive growth in governmental regulation agencies. There are over 75,000 governmental employees engaged in promulgating regulations, at a cost to the nation estimated conservatively at $60 billion. Recently, the San Francisco regional office wrote to school administrators in Scottsdale, Arizona, that according to a ruling by the Department of Health, Education and Welfare, the father-son and mother-daughter events in public schools violate the sex discrimination policy, and could result in a cutoff of federal funds.

Our national debt should be a cause of grave concern. It seems that the maxim, "a penny saved is a penny earned," has yielded to the slogan, "spend now, pay later." The debt limit, officially set at $400 billion, is "temporarily" increased by Congress. Today, the debt is $616 billion with interest payments annually of $37.4 billion. It is estimated that by 1982 the debt will be one trillion dollars, with interest charges to the taxpayers of $65 billion. It appears that some politicians callously promise what they know they cannot deliver, and try to deceive the people into believing that projects can always be paid for out of somebody else's pocket. We must protect ourselves not only against external enemies, but also against enemies within our nation whose recklessness can lead us into bankruptcy.

We are concerned that the communications media, which has the power to shape society, tends to exercise that power irresponsibly. In the past decade, television programming reflects an increased use of gutter language, of excessive violence, and of semi-raw sex. Don Johnston, President of the large advertising agency, J. Walter Thompson Company, reporting the findings of a pilot research, said: "Public hostility to violent programming is growing; it is organizing, and I am convinced it will make itself felt more and more." The preliminary survey revealed that as many as one-fifth of the men and one-third of the women do not permit their children to view objectionable programs, and 8% of the respondents consciously do not purchase products advertised on such programs. He said his agency is obliged to counsel its clients that certain programs turn off potential buyers. Some spokesmen for the TV industry allege that they are merely giving people what they want, that they simply mirror the mores of society. It is for the viewers to prove that bad morality can make bad business, and that the police blotter does not accurately mirror the mores of the entire community.

President Eisenhower, with good reason, warned us about the military-industrial complex. The arms race is a treacherous trap for humanity. It is not the only way and certainly not the best way to secure an enduring peace. As a nation, we must be strong and always prepared to defend ourselves against unjust aggressors. However, we must direct our efforts and resources towards bilateral disarmament agreements, backed by authentic and workable safeguards. Peace must be born of mutual trust. It cannot be imposed by fear of one another's weapons.

Our concern derives from the current reversal of the downward trend of military spending, which prevailed since 1968. The proposal for spending $101 billion for fiscal year 1977 is but a first step in a proposed arms buildup. This buildup calls for a 4% annual increase for the next five years, to a total of $141 billion in fiscal year 1981 — not including the costly overruns. Additionally, the Pentagon is worried that the profits of weapon makers are not high enough and is seeking ways to increase them. This buildup is based on an assumption that the matching of military weapons is the only adequate means of defense. It is men and not weapons that wage and win wars. The buildup of military weapons is a sure way of dissipating our national resources and weakening our strength.

These are but some of our concerns as we cross the threshold of the third century of our national life. These concerns are serious but not overwhelming. They call for continued vigilance and effort. We are, after all, a government of the people, by the people and for the people. Governments do respond to the will of the people. We must not tolerate that which is wrong, and our silence can be a vote for wrong. The Swiss author, Henri F. Amiel, said: "Truth is violated by falsehood, but is outraged by silence." Shakespeare expressed the same thought in the words: "A little fire is quickly trodden out which, being suffered, rivers cannot quench."

Today we must rededicate ourselves to the beliefs and principles which guided our Founding Fathers. We must work and pray that this nation under God — this government, of, by, and for the people shall not perish. With confidence, we must pray: "May your kindness, O Lord, be upon us who have put our hope in you."

We Pray that America Will Return to Its Spiritual Foundations

Broadcast on WFIL Radio on December 27, 1976, December 31, 1976.

As we begin the third century in our one nation under God, we thank Him for past blessings, ask His mercy and forgiveness for our sins and failings, and seek His guidance for the future. Our Declaration of Independence articulates the principles that the spiritual is supreme and that man is of divine origin. Our rights to life, liberty, and the pursuit of happiness have their foundation in our God-given human dignity.

We pray that in the third century, the condition of religious and moral decline will be reversed. We must be as firm in encouraging the teaching of religious and moral principles as we are decisive in denying tax funds for the teaching of sectarian doctrine.

Jefferson said that "as government grows, freedom recedes." We pray that before long the people of our nation will seek ways to contain the explosive growth of governmental regulatory agencies which operate at a cost of sixty billion dollars to American taxpayers.

History tells us that many great nations have died at their own hands. It is my prayer that certain trends that invite self-destruction will be reversed in the next 100 years; that America will return to its spiritual foundations, and, above all, respect human life, which is our nation's most prized possession and most valuable natural resource.

Protecting Human Rights Everywhere in the World

Homily at the Mass at the Sixth Annual Polish Festival, on June 5, 1977.

I speak to you today on a subject that is quite current; a subject which frequently finds its way into the headlines, into articles, into editorials, and that is the subject of human rights.

We know that the Second Vatican Council brought into bold relief the insistence on the dignity of man and on the sacredness of human rights. It was at the Synod of 1974 in Rome that the Holy Father together with the bishops assembled in that Synod issued a message on human rights. The message said that no nation today is faultless where human rights are concerned. It called upon all to promote human rights and to give hope to those who suffer violation of their rights. In that brief message special attention is given to: first, the right to life which is being violated today by abortion, euthanasia, torture, acts of violence against innocent parties, the scourge of war. Secondly, the right to eat. Millions in the world today are undernourished. Millions face starvation, and die of it. The third was politico-cultural rights and the message insisted that individuals should have an effective role in shaping their own destinies. They have a right to participate in the political process freely and responsibly. They have the right as well as the freedom of dissent. They have a right to be educated and to determine the education of their children. They have a right to be secure from arrest, torture, imprisonment for political or ideological reasons. And the fifth caption was the right of religious liberty. Today this right is denied or restricted by diverse political systems in ways which impede worship, religious education and social ministry. And the message says, "We call upon all governments to acknowledge the right of religious liberty in words and foster it in deeds, to eliminate any type of discrimination, and to accord to all, regardless of their religious convictions, the full rights and opportunities of citizens."

Deep appreciation of human rights

We affirm our determination to foster human rights and reconciliation everywhere in the Church and the world today. Why do I speak to you about human rights? Actually, the history of Poland has a brilliant jewel, a document submitted by Pawel Wodkiewicz to the Council of Constance. That document came to full expression 500 years later in the Second Vatican Council's declaration on religious liberty. It has been a long Polish tradition that the violation of human rights anywhere in the world was the concern of everybody. And it was that kind of a conviction that brought Tadeusz Kosciuszko to these shores to fight according to the motto of Poland: "For your and our freedom." There has been a deep appreciation of human rights throughout the history of Poland.

We can go back another 300 years to the Statutes of Kalisz in 1254. This federal statute made it a crime, severely punishable, for defacing a Jewish synagogue, a Jewish cemetery, or in any way taking actions against the Jewish residents of Poland. These statutes are a matter of historical record.

Even before the Magna Carta was signed in England, there was a document which bound the nobility to respect the rights of the peasants in Poland. Human rights is something which is a part of us, and the importance of it in the life of every Pole is something that cannot be gainsaid. Life does not hold importance if there is no freedom.

In 1939, a few days before war broke out in Poland, I was walking in the uplands, as they call them, the "Pod Karpaty" section from which my dad emigrated. At this time, practically all the manpower and the horsepower had been drafted in preparation for the war which did take place in a matter of days. I ran into three relatively young men. They had been to the village tavern. They were returning to their homes. They were married men, with families and children. On the eve of their departure for the army, they greeted me deferentially. I asked them, "You are going to war. Do you think you have a chance?" And they looked at me in astonishment! "That does not make a bit of difference! We must fight, chance or no chance!" I said, "What will happen should you be attacked from the rear, by the Soviets?" "Then we will be fighting two devils instead of one."

The ideology of these people is absolutely unbelievable, and yet, that is the ideology which has a tradition of almost a thousand years in Poland.

Taking to heart the establishment of greater justice

The Church spoke about human rights in a specific message in 1974. The Church does not have an army. It cannot impose its way. But moral persuasion is a factor in human life. I do not say that the Church's message of 1974 was the sole cause for the Helsinki meeting, but the reality is that on August 1, 1975, there was an accord reached at Helsinki with 35 nations, including the Vatican, in which the nations pledged to respect fundamental rights, including the right of religious freedom. The Communist countries agreed to open gradually their closed societies, and to permit freer exchange of ideas and information with the West. There was to be closer contact between peoples of the Communist and Western Worlds—more freedom to travel, to meet, to talk without government interference.

It would be pessimistic to say that the accord has not produced good results. And it would be untrue to say that all of the agreements have been respected. They have not. In spite of the Helsinki Agreement, Radio Free Europe is still being jammed, and the truth—freedom of expression—is not being recognized in Czechoslovakia, Bulgaria, Poland. The people are being insulated against any information from the outside. In Czechoslovakia, the propaganda chief said: "The party does not ascribe any mystical importance to the conclusions reached at Helsinki. Any overestimation of them could lead to unjustified illusions; any such illusions could be very dangerous and harmful."

And we know that one of the party officials of Russia said that the Helsinki Agreement can in no way interfere with the ideology of the Communist party.

But, we still speak out. The bishops of America have been eloquent and actually, under the chairmanship of our Bishop Dougherty, the Commission on Justice and Peace in the World has spoken out strongly and positively. The Holy Father is doing that. Just two months ago, on April 4th, in receiving the credentials of the Iranian Ambassador, he said: "The Holy See carries the responsibility for a message of universal well-being. It takes to heart the rights of persons and peoples so that in liberty, justice and equality, they might reach the conditions which human development requires." And he said that all men must be firmly determined to consolidate through peace, which goes hand-in-hand with the advancement of human rights, the establishment of greater justice for everyone, and help to places and peoples less fortunate.

There is another great churchman who is speaking out for human rights, eloquently, forcefully and wisely. Just a month ago on May 3rd, at the Marian Shrine of Our Lady of Czestochowa in Poland, the Cardinal Primate of Poland, Cardinal Wyszynski, said, "It is not enough to pray for religious liberty." He said, "While we have rights, we also have the obligation to demand that in our nation believers have the protection of law." He urged Catholics to remind law enforcers that each man should be assured that his ties to the Church, and his wish to profess Christ's Gospel, will be respected always. He urged all the Poles to assert their rights and to give their children a religious education. He said, "We cannot be made to become atheists in our country through force, through violence or through a situation in which children hear nothing in schools about Jesus, the Gospel, or the history of the Church in Poland." He charged the government with trying to replace the Church's sacramental system and its rituals with secular ceremonies. He said, "No one can replace by force our sacramental system with secular ceremonies, which for Catholics and Christians have no meaning. The bottom line of any discussion on justice and peace must be respect for human rights."

We are dealing internationally with an integrated philosophy of Communism. The constitutions of Communist nations do have the words guaranteeing freedom of expression. In fact, just yesterday there was released a new draft of a constitution in the Soviet Union. This first revision of the 1936 Constitutional Charter of Joseph Stalin, like its predecessor, repeats the declaration about the guarantees of freedom of speech, assembly, religion, and other ostensible privileges, but it also adds the exercise of rights and freedom shall be inseparable from the performance by citizens of their duties. It mentions obligations of all religious beliefs to Soviet laws. But we must ask: How can a system that has declared war to death against religion and religious beliefs say that it does recognize something which it intends to destroy? Let us look at the record. Let's stop listening to the promises of Communism, and let's look at their record of performance.

Atheism vs. belief in God

Poland, for almost thirty years, has been the battlefield of the two greatest ideologies of the world—atheism and belief in God. The government has control of the press, of the electronic media, of education, and of most of the charitable institutions. It exercises a real tight control on printing, and duplicating materials. The Church has only a limited press and a limited opportunity of communications. And yet, after thirty years, that atheistic campaign has not succeeded. Not only is the faith of the people of Poland preserved, but the Church in Poland is strong. Today, over a thousand missionaries have left Poland in the past dozen years to serve in different parts of the world. Poland is helping the faith in other areas.

The atheistic campaign is not succeeding. We cannot panic or be scared by the progress of Communism. It has made tremendous progress. It has since the last world war extended its control from 7 to 35 percent of the world's population, from 18 to 25 percent of the land area of the world. It has made progress. But, has it sold its doctrine to the people? That's another question. The fact is the campaign of atheism is not successful.

Communism says it is for the proletariat — for the workingman — and according to the doctrine of Marx, it is the workingman who must have the ownership, the control, and the use of the means of production. Communism is anti-capitalistic. But what has it achieved? It has merely exchanged private capitalism for State capitalism.

To this day, after sixty years of experience, the workingman in the Communist nations does not own the means of production. He does not control it, and he does not have use of it for his own benefit. Communism has conducted a systematic, intensive anti-religion campaign. Has it succeeded? It hasn't.

Hunger for God

When Svetlana Alliluyeva, the daughter of Stalin, came to the United States, one of the first things that she had to do was embrace a religion. She made some beautiful statements that she could not live without God. While she had been totally isolated from any religious instruction or influences, yet when she came to the United States the greatest hunger that she had was for God, for religion. And there are young people today in Russia under Soviet domination who are bearing witness to the truth of what St. Augustine said fifteen centuries ago, "You have created us for You, O Lord, and our hearts are restless until they repose in You." Communism has not succeeded in exterminating a sense of religion. Furthermore, the Marxist system of collectivism makes the State all-important and makes the individual subject to the demands and the needs of the State. Because the existence of God is denied, no man can claim the God-given rights which our Constitution declares and protects. And secondly, because the State is important, the individual then becomes a servant, a slave of the State. That is the controlling philosophic principle of Marxism. For example, in the eighty years of Russian Czarism there were about eighty people executed a year. In the '37, '38, '39 disturbances under Stalin in Russia, there were 40,000 a month executed in Russia. Earlier in the twenties, there was an artificially created famine which called for the extermination, the death, of some six million peasants in the Ukraine. That was supposed to set straight the whole economy. So these people became expendable. Communism was the first in the history of the world to introduce the slave labor camps, the Siberian camps;

the first to introduce the practice of putting people on barges and sending them out to the open sea to be drowned; the first one to introduce an artificial type of registration so that the State can have full control of every individual. It was the first to introduce the system of hostages. If they could not reach an individual, they would reach his wife, his children, his parents. The suppression and repression of human rights is not an accident of the system of Communist philosophy. It is a normal fruit and a normal product of such a philosophy. For that reason, when we read about the guarantee of human rights under the Marxist system, we should understand that there are always the qualifications that collectivism and the State are more important than the individual. Since Marxists deny the existence of God, they must deny the claim of any human being that he has God-given rights, which governments must respect.

I speak to you about this today—and perhaps too long—but it is important for us, as Americans, to appreciate the freedom that we have here. It is important for us as Americans and Catholics to understand what is taking place not only in Poland, but in all areas occupied by the integrated, philosophical system called Marxism.

We are gathered here today, most of us Poles, most of us indebted for our religious and cultural heritage to Poland. I have tried, not by denunciation, to explain some principles and some realities, bearing on human rights. The first reason why we are here in this stadium is this altar. In the long tradition of Poland, in every trial, in every need, in every joy and every sorrow, Poles were at the altar begging God and His Blessed Mother. And just in case you are wondering, this extremely beautiful chasuble is one which was presented to me at the time of the Eucharistic Congress by the bishops of Poland with the hope that it might inspire people to intensify their prayers to the Blessed Mother. This year we celebrate the sixtieth year of the apparitions of Our Lady of Fatima, which occurred even before the Bolshevik revolution of October, 1917. She had predicted what was going to happen. She asked for prayers. So we are assembled here for prayers, and I beg of you, my dear brothers and sisters, that during this Eucharistic Sacrifice you do offer prayers to Almighty God for the protection of human rights everywhere in the world, but especially for religious freedom — freedom for the Church — in our beloved ancestral home of Poland. God bless you.

Attending to the Pastoral Needs of Immigrants

Address, "Del Primer Encuentro Nacional Hispano de Pastoral al Segundo Encuentro," on August 19, 1977.

Five years ago it was my privilege to convoke the *Primer Encuentro Hispano de Pastoral*, and to celebrate and to deliver the homily in Spanish at the opening Liturgy. The deliberations of the 1973 Encuentro produced 78 conclusions. The report submitted to you evinces that at least 60% of the recommendations have been implemented in the intervening five years.

Such unprecedented "instant" success in progress is attributable above all to the sympathetic concern and disposition of the National Conference of Catholic Bishops, as well as to the energetic leadership of its Ad Hoc Committee for Spanish-Speaking under the able chairmanship of Bishop Rausch, as well as to the NCCB Secretariat under the zealous leadership of its Director, Mr. Paul Sedillo, Jr.

Leadership is vital and indispensable for the success of any project, but the best leadership must depend upon an interested and determined constituency, willing to make sacrifices of time, talent and energy for the cause. In this perspective, the successes of the past five years are attributable not only to the bishops—their Conference, their Ad Hoc Committee and their Secretariat—but also to the Regional and Diocesan Pastoral Centers for Hispanics, and to the enthusiastic cooperation of all involved with these various organizations.

I shall not attempt to report in detail the implementation of the conclusions of the *Primer Encuentro Hispano de Pastoral.* You have the printed report on implementation prepared by the NCCB/USCC Secretariat for the Spanish-Speaking. I prefer to share with you some reflections on why the progress you made was possible.

The Church's solicitude for migrants

The answer to this question is found in the long record of the Church's solicitude for migrants. The Church, striving to fulfill the duties inherent in her Christ-given mandate of sanctification and salvation for all mankind, has been especially careful to provide spiritual care for pilgrims, aliens, exiles and migrants. The Church proposes the emigré Holy Family of Nazareth seeking refuge in the foreign land of Egypt as a prototype of every migrant family. The Church echoes the words of our Lord: "I was a stranger and you welcomed me" (Mt. 26:35), and Paul's "be generous in offering hospitality," (Rom. 13:13), and translates them into a program of action.

St. Augustine of Hippo insistently urged priests to provide the victims of oppressive catastrophies with spiritual care. St. Ambrose sold sacred vessels to ransom captives. Religious orders, congregations and pious associations were founded and flourished throughout the Christian world to provide for strangers. Pilgrims' halls and hospices were established.

Experience proved that the most effective ministry among strangers was carried on by priests of their own nationality, or at least by priests who spoke their language. The Fourth Lateran Council in 1215 affirmed:

"In most countries, we find cities and dioceses in which people of diverse languages, though bound by one faith, have various rites and customs. Therefore, we strictly enjoin that the bishops of these cities or dioceses provide the proper men who will celebrate the liturgical functions according to their own rites and languages" (c. IX). This instruction has been repeatedly affirmed in various Church documents and applied in practice to our own days.

The Second Vatican Council explicitly affirmed and expanded this instruction in its documents. The Decree on Bishops called for special concern for migrants, exiles, refugees and others who cannot sufficiently make use of the common and ordinary pastoral services of parish priests. Episcopal conferences were enjoined to pay energetic attention to the more pressing problems confronted by such groups (no. 18). The post-conciliar Directory of Pastoral

Ministry of Bishops directed bishops to promote diligently the spiritual care of migrants and their families according to the norms laid down by the Council and the Apostolic See (no. 156).

Thus, the response of the National Conference of Catholic Bishops to conclusions and recommendations of the *Primer Encuentro Nacional* is consistent with and called for by the mission of the Church and the instructions and practice of the Holy See.

"A teeming nation of nations"

The United States is a country of immigrants. In the words of Walt Whitman, it "is not merely a nation but a teeming nation of nations." According to available records only the Redmen — the Indians — are natives. Since 1607, when the first English settlers landed at Jamestown, Virginia, more than sixty million people have migrated to the United States — the largest mass migration in recorded history.

Because the United States is predominantly an English-speaking nation, there has been an impression that the English immigrants alone cleared the forests primeval, fought the Revolution, secured independence — and then the "others" — Irish, Germans, Jews, Hispanics — began to arrive. These "others" were regarded by some as foreigners, not always welcome, often discriminated against and sometimes persecuted.

These impressions are not supported by facts, by the record. Before the pilgrims landed in

Plymouth in 1620, six sturdy Poles, on September 25, 1608, started a glass furnace, the first factory in the Jamestown Colony. These Poles went on strike and won an instant victory, not for wages, but for civil rights. They struck because the governor of the colony declared that only natives of England would be allowed to vote. The Court Book of the Virginia Company records: "Upon some dispute of the Polonians ...it was now agreed that they shall be enfranchised and made as free as any inhabitant."

When in 1664 the English took possession of the Hudson River Valley Colony, originally settled by the Dutch, they found eighteen different nationalities and almost as many religions. One of the major grievances cited in the Declaration of Independence was the discrimination against non-English immigrants: "He [King George III] has endeavored to prevent the population of these States; for that reason obstructing the Laws of Naturalization of Foreigners; refusing to pass others to encourage their migrations hither."

It should be noted that eighteen of the fifty-six signers of the Declaration of Independence were of non-English stock and eight were first-generation immigrants.

It is unfortunate that some people tend to see the worst and to be suspicious of strangers, newcomers, foreigners. History records the cruel lash of prejudice directed against Catholics in the seventeenth and eighteenth centuries. In Maryland, anti-Catholic legislation attempted to curtail Catholic immigration through a system of excessive duties and penalty fees and to dispossess Catholics who had settled in Maryland.

In the nineteenth century the Great Famine in Ireland brought a tidal wave of desperate humanity to the shores of the United States. The anti-Catholic, anti-foreign hostility took political form in various organizations in the Nativist movements, which gave rise to the American party—nicknamed the "Know-Nothings." Inflamed by a spirit of intolerance, the Nativists caused the explosion of anti-Irish riots in Philadelphia and New York. Mobs attacked Catholic churches in Philadelphia, Clinton and Southbridge, Massachusetts and Raritan. Sisters of Charity were assaulted in Providence, Rhode Island. The "Know-Nothings" pledged to rid the country of foreign influence, and in 1855 elected six state governors and seventy-five Congressmen, and in 1856 won 25% of the presidential vote.

The anti-foreign sentiment declined but did not disappear after the Civil War. It crested in the Chinese Exclusion Act of 1882, which in an effort to fight the so-called "Yellow Peril" closed the door to Chinese immigrants and denied citizenship to natives of China. At the turn of the century, such organizations as the anti-Catholic American Protective Association, the Immigration Restriction League and the Japanese and Korean Exclusion League lobbied furiously against the noble sentiments expressed by the silent lips of the Statue of Liberty—the Mother of Exiles—sculptured by the Italian Auguste Bartholdi, in the words of the sonnet composed by Emma Lazarus, descendant of Spanish Jews: "Give me your tired, your poor, your huddled masses yearning to breathe free, the wretched refuse of your teeming shores."

The climax of agitation against the immigrant came in 1916 in the publication of Madison Grant's *The Passing of the Great Race*, in which he lamented the decline of the Anglo-Saxon and Nordic supermen of the universe, and the influx of races drawn from the "lowest stratum of the Mediterranean basin and the Balkans," whom he described as the "human flotsam, and the whole tone of American life—social, moral and political —has been lowered and vulgarized by them."

The Immigration Acts of 1920 and 1924 used a "national origin" system that was shamelessly based on the racist theory of Grant. The Immigration and Nationality Act of 1952 was passed by Congress over the veto of President Truman who objected: "The idea behind this discriminatory policy was, to put it boldly, that Americans with English or Irish names were better people and better citizens than Americans with Italian or Greek or Polish names.... Such a concept is utterly unworthy of our traditions and our ideals."

It was on October 3, 1965, that President Johnson, at the foot of the Statue of Liberty, signed into law a new immigration bill which declared that the government of the United States was determined to apply in practice our ideals of equality and freedom. The last vestige of discrimination against the "foreigner" has been removed from the books. Regrettably, the sentiment of anti-foreign discrimination has not been excised from the hearts of men by the new law. Some of this sentiment surfaced with the immigration of the South Vietnamese.

The Church of immigrants

The Church in the United States is a Church of immigrants. Its history begins with the discovery of America and the assignment of missionaries to the Spanish, the French and the English colonies. The Bull, *Sublimis Deus,* of Pope Paul III, June 2, 1537, affirmed the traditional teaching of the Catholic Church concerning the spiritual equality and brotherhood of all men, with special reference to the conversion of the Indians — the Redmen.

John Carroll, the first bishop of the United States, in a pastoral letter expressed the thought uppermost in his mind by exhorting the faithful that it was "their duty to erect a church suitable to their needs."

The recently canonized St. John Neumann — the fourth bishop of Philadelphia — provides a classic example of the Church's solicitude for the immigrant. He was recommended for the office of bishop of Philadelphia by the great scholar and orator, Bishop Kenrick. John Neumann was an unlikely candidate for the office of bishop of the then-largest diocese.

He was an immigrant, small in stature, who spoke with a heavy accent. He could not match the eloquence of his predecessors in office. However, his appointment made it clear that the Church in the United States was indeed a Church of immigrants. He spoke German and the Slavic languages. He invited the Italians to services in his own chapel, and subsequently established the first Italian parish in Philadelphia, and probably in the United States. He studied Gaelic and ministered to the Irish immigrants in their native language. St. John Neumann provides us with a classic example of the Church's solicitude for the immigrant.

However, more eloquent than any historical records and than any words of mine are the living monuments—the national or language and rite churches, parishes, schools and seminaries. With the encouragement of the first bishop, John Carroll, and under the direction of their local ordinaries, the immigrants, while struggling for a foothold in the new country, and generally living on the lowest economic rung of the social ladder, made tremendous sacrifices to build churches, schools and other institutions to meet their own needs. Some of the national churches erected are in many respects larger and more magnificent than some present-day cathedrals. The Germans established the Josephinum Seminary in Columbus, Ohio, and the Poles, Sts. Cyril and Methodius Seminary in Orchard Lake, Michigan. The Bohemians still have their Benedictine Abbey in Lisle, Illinois, and the Slovaks have theirs in Cleveland, Ohio. The Ukrainians and the Ruthenians have their own seminaries.

These parochial and other ecclesiastical institutions built by the immigrants bear witness to the Church's solicitude for the immigrant and the Church's desire to have their respective cultural and religious heritages preserved and integrated into the culture of the new world.

Perhaps one of the greatest evidences of the Church's concern for immigrants and refugees was the Montezuma Seminary, built in the United States by the American hierarchy for young Mexican aspirants to the priesthood. When in this century the faithful in Mexico were persecuted and fled to the United States, Pope Benedict XV in letters to the bishop of San Antonio and the Archbishop of Baltimore proposed a seminary for young Mexican seminarians. The bishops of the United States responded generously by building a special seminary for Mexicans in the Archdiocese of Santa Fe. The seminary continued until the last decade. It was discontinued only because there were enough seminaries opened in Mexico to provide for the needs of the Church.

It is an undisputable fact, supported by deeds and documents, that the Church did not subscribe to the "Nativist" concept of the assimilation of cultures—the Melting-Pot theory—but sought to provide for the preservation and integration of the various cultures.

I have said that you have made gratifying progress since the *Primer Encuentro*. In fact, the more than fifty-five year history of the Conference of Bishops in the United States does not record another instance of an Ad Hoc Committee, or a Conference Secretariat for a particular language group. You should be pleased and gratified with such success and progress.

ATTENDING TO THE PASTORAL NEEDS OF IMMIGRANTS 241

Invoking God's guidance and blessings upon the discussions of this *Segundo Encuentro*, I urge you to contain all of your deliberations within the framework of your theme of evangelization, with special emphasis on the pastoral needs of the Hispanics within the Church's mission of sanctification and salvation in our Lord Jesus Christ.

Setting a Pro-Life Trend in Our Society

Letter read at all Masses on Respect Life Sunday, October 2, 1977.

Dear Friends of Life:

Human life is a gift from Almighty God. God created man in His divine image (Gn. 1:27). The Psalmist praises God: "Truly, you have formed my inmost being—you knit me in my mother's womb" (139:13). Job repeats that God forms and fashions us before our birth (10:8, 11; 31:15). The prophet Jeremiah quotes the Lord: "Before I formed you in the womb, I knew you, before you were born I dedicated you, a prophet to the nations I appointed you" (1:4).

The gift of human life is present in the womb—before birth. This has been the conviction of humankind for centuries; this is the clear finding of science. Neither sentiment nor semantics can obscure the fact that the child in the womb has received God's gift of life; or that the destruction of such human life—whether by scorching with chemicals or dismembering with surgical instruments—is unspeakable cruelty and a crime against the unborn child and against

God. Human life, at every moment of its growth and development, must be respected and protected.

Our respect for human life is unconditional. We do not ask whether a human life is wanted or unwanted; whether it is or is not productive; whether it can or cannot contribute to social, economic or political welfare. We respect human life because it is, because it lives, because it is a gift of God—a work of His creation. The right to life is so fundamental that it is inalienable and cannot be superseded by any other right.

Unfortunately, respect for human life is threatened in many areas. One sees the waste of human life through dissolute living; the waste of a human mind through laziness or incompetence; the waste of a human person through careless accidents. There is the waste of human spirit sapped by hunger and poverty. Sometimes, there is the waste of life itself through abortion. There are the future threats to non-productive human life such as the killing of the elderly and the handicapped. As difficult as it is to believe, a recent newspaper headline stated: "Let the retarded infants die."

As Christians who believe in a loving God and in His loving care for all mankind, we must be signs of respect for life. We must be aware of our personal responsibility to live our lives knowing that they are gifts from God. We must consider the lives of others, no matter who they are, as gifts from God. We can begin by treating persons as more important than things, and by demanding that society around us do the same.

244 TO INSURE PEACE ACKNOWLEDGE GOD

We must become more aware of trends in our society which lessen respect for all human life. But, more importantly, we must set a pro-life trend in our society by responding to human needs through service, compassion and love for our brothers and sisters who have their life from God, our Father.

On the Panama Canal Treaties

Statement on behalf of the United States Catholic Conference, Washington, D.C., accompanied by Rev. J. Bryan Hehir, Director, Office of International Justice and Peace, United States Catholic Conference, Washington, D.C., on October 10-14, 1977.

Mr. Chairman and members of the committee, I am, as you have announced, John Cardinal Krol, Archbishop of Philadelphia. My companion here at the table is Father J. Bryan Hehir, director of the Office of Foreign Affairs of the United States Catholic Conference.

My testimony is given in the name of the United States Catholic Conference, which is the civil action agency of the more than 330 Catholic bishops of our country who serve close to 50 million people in our country.

At the outset, Mr. Chairman, I wish to express my deep personal appreciation and that of the United States Catholic Conference for the opportunity to present testimony in support of the proposed Panama Canal Treaties.

Catholic bishops' interest in need for new treaty

The Catholic bishops took an early stand and an interest in the need for a new treaty; in February of 1975, the Administrative Board of the Conference adopted a policy position supporting the Kissinger-Tack agreements of 1974 and called for a new treaty to govern relationships between the United States and Panama.

In November, 1976, the general meeting of the bishops adopted a second statement endorsing the need for a new treaty.

We regard this question as one of great symbolic and substantive significance for the peoples and nations of the Western Hemisphere. We also recognize that the treaties are a subject on which American citizens hold strong and differing views.

In the 1976 debate in the bishops' conference on our second policy statement, it was illustrated that there were some differences of views among the bishops on specific aspects of our position, even though the position was adopted by a vote of 170 to 61.

My testimony today is based on the major themes of the two policy positions taken by the Catholic bishops in support of the new treaty with Panama.

In presenting this testimony, the bishops wish to fulfill a role of responsible citizenship as well as religious leadership. We come here not to express a doctrine of faith, but to draw upon a Catholic social teaching to highlight the moral dimensions of this very significant public debate taking place in our nation.

Requirement of justice and peace

In our 1976 statement, the bishops asserted that a moral imperative existed

to fashion a new treaty which respects the territorial integrity and sovereignty of Panama, and dissolves the vestiges of a relationship which more closely resembles the 19th century than the realities of an interdependent world of sovereign and equal states.

I came here today, Mr. Chairman, to express our convictions that the treaties now before this committee achieve the objectives called for in our 1976 statement.

It was our view in 1975 and 1976, and it is our view today, that a new treaty which acknowledges in principle and in fact Panamanian sovereignty over its own territory is a requirement of justice and peace between our two nations. It is a requirement of justice because the 1903 treaty no longer can be reconciled with the concept of social justice which governs relations between sovereign nations in our interdependent world. It is a requirement of peace because we believe failure to reach a reasonable and just accommodation of interests between our nations needlessly threatens the peace in this hemisphere.

In support of these propositions, I respectfully submit a series of considerations which specify the points of justice and peace at issue in this case of the Panama Canal. We hope these will be of assistance to this committee, to the

Senate in its deliberations, and to American citizens as they consider this question.

Our perspective on the treaty negotiations and now on the treaties themselves has been set by a text from Pope John XXIII's encyclical on international relations, *Peace on Earth*.

In his discussion of relations between States, Pope John said:

> Each of them, accordingly, is vested with the right to existence, to self-development and the means fitting to its attainment, and to be the one primarily responsible for this self-development.

The terms of the 1903 treaty acknowledge the principle of Panamanian sovereignty, but prevent its exercise in any form in the Canal Zone. Such a restriction on sovereignty, imposed from the outside, makes it impossible for Panama either to realize its right to self-development or to be the principal agent of its destiny in the world community.

This is the key moral issue at stake in these treaties.

It is important to note at this point, Mr. Chairman, that Catholic teaching on international relations does not give political sovereignty an absolute moral value. At a deeper level than political or legal sovereignty is the reality of human community, which happens to be shaped at this stage of history by a world of States. There are basic human responsibilities among people and nations which we think take precedence over the legal claims of States. At the same time, it is in our view necessary to acknowledge a real, if relative, value to the concept of sovereignty in the world of States.

The legitimate claims of sovereignty make it possible for a State in a still disorganized world to protect the fundamental rights of its people against outside interference and to marshal the resources and energies of its national heritage for the good of its people.

These are objectives which touch the very identity and dignity as well as the socio-economic welfare of a country. They are objectives which we take for granted as the right of our own nation in the world. Yet, under the provisions of the 1903 treaty, these minimal objectives of a State are severely restricted by us in the case of Panama.

It is this prevailing situation which cries out for redress. The great opportunity of the moment, Mr. Chairman, an opportunity of both justice and peace, is that we can redress the situation by the democratic procedure of a vote in this legislative body of the United States. It is our hope and prayer, Mr. Chairman, that the significance of this moment will not be lost in the intensity of debate presently surrounding this issue.

Symbolic significance of moment

The substantive significance is the issue of political and legal justice I have just specified. But the symbolic significance of the moment is no less important: One of the largest and one of the smallest nations of the world have been dangerously close to conflict for over a decade;

it is now possible to lay this conflict to rest and in so doing to provide an example in world affairs of how States of very different political, economic, and military power can deal with each other in terms of equality, dignity, and mutual respect.

There are too few examples of this kind in the world today. It would be a political and a moral tragedy of the first order if we were to squander this opportunity.

Complementing this dimension of political-legal justice, there is a second moral question at stake in a new treaty. Sovereignty is a political concept, but in world politics today the implications of sovereignty have significant socio-economic consequences.

In both our 1975 and 1976 statements on United States-Panama relations, we stressed how present restrictions on Panamanian sovereignty substantially retard the possibilities for economic development in that nation. We say this even while we readily acknowledge that the existence of the canal, built and operated under U.S. auspices, has brought substantial economic benefit to Panama in this century.

The acknowledgement of this fact should not, however, overshadow the equally relevant truth that the existing inability of Panama to integrate the canal and territory comprising the Canal Zone into its national planning has serious long-term economic consequences, ranging from urban congestion in Panama City to the level of revenue which Panama can gain from operating the canal.

The political issue of restrictions on Panamanian sovereignty strikes at national pride and dignity. The economic issue resulting from restrictions on Panamanian sovereignty strikes at the human dignity and economic welfare of the people of Panama.

It is a stated policy goal of our nation to foster the political and economic development of the nations of the Third World. In the treaties now before this committee, the potential exists to make a significant contribution to one of those nations by opening the possibility for more rational and comprehensive economic planning through restoring to Panamanian control the precious 500-plus square miles of territory which now bisects that country.

The remarks I have made thus far bring me to two concluding considerations. One bears upon our relations with others, and the second upon our perception of ourselves as a nation.

Symbolic significance of treaties

I have already commented upon the symbolic significance of these treaties, but the idea is worthy of a final reflection.

In the increasingly interdependent world of which we are a part, our relations with the nations of the developing world will be both complex and of considerable importance. The way those relations are shaped will have a decisive impact on what Pope John called the international common good.

The Panama Canal Treaties constitute a prismatic case of how decisions among individual nations can contribute to the international common good. All the political and economic dynamics involved between the industrialized and developing nations are reflected in this issue.

We are being observed closely for signs of how we respond to these dynamics in a concrete case. There is a significant opportunity here for the United States and Panama to signal a new kind of relationship between large and small, industrialized and developing nations. Nothing would signify the meaning of this new relationship more vividly than the resolution of this emotionally laden problem by the stroke of the pen rather than strife between our nations.

The opportunity, however, is not confined to contributing to the international common good. It is our considered judgment, Mr. Chairman, that these treaties also achieve for the United States the basic national interest we have in a canal which is open and efficiently operated. Other witnesses will testify in detail about the political, strategic, and economic dimensions of the treaties. As bishops, we bring no special technical competence to these discussions, and therefore have not stressed technical issues in this testimony.

In preparing this statement, however, we have considered these elements, including the specific point we made in our 1976 statement, that the welfare of the people living and working in the Canal Zone be given just consideration.

We are of the opinion that this question and other legitimate national interests of the United

States in a new treaty have been provided for in the texts now before this committee.

Argument that United States will appear weak

We are aware that some who oppose the ratification of the treaties use an argument that in accepting a new treaty relationship the United States will appear to be weak or in retreat. This assertion deserves comment, because it touches directly on how we think of ourselves as a nation, on how we conceive the values which structure our identity, and on how we wish to project ourselves in the world community.

It is our view, Mr. Chairman, that the treaties provide us with an opportunity to project an image of strength which derives from the strongest dimension of our national heritage—not our military might, but the values and principles which are the foundation of our identity as a people.

We are a nation born of the desire to be free from foreign domination; the concepts of liberty and self-determination are woven through the fabric of our history. It is these values which are synonymous with our political philosophy. When we affirm the values of liberty and self-determination for ourselves and for others, we speak from the most significant strain of our national heritage.

Our commitment to those values is perceived by others not only in terms of whether we are determined to preserve them for ourselves, but also whether we are willing to affirm them in our relations with other States, especially those smaller and less powerful than we are.

In the past we have been willing to take up arms in defense of liberty and self-determination; today, in this case of the Panama Canal Treaties, we can affirm the values by a peaceful act of national will in ratifying what our President has signed.

In the past we have stood for the principle of nonintervention by others in the Western Hemisphere. Today we are asked to manifest our commitment to the principle of nonintervention by an act of self-restraint and forebearance included in these treaties.

It is of the essence of national strength to be confident about the values which are at the heart of a nation's life and to be guided by those values in moments of great importance. We have such a moment before us, and we can prove our strength by affirming for others what we most prize in our national life.

Thank you, Mr. Chairman, and thank you, members of the committee.

Resolutely Safeguarding Human Life

Keynote address at the Respect Life Educational Workshop, April 27, 1978.

Pastoral plan for pro-life activities

In 1975, the Catholic bishops of the United States issued a three-phase Pastoral Plan for Pro-Life Activities. The first phase calls for an educational-public information effort to inform, clarify, and deepen understanding of the basic pro-life issues. This workshop is an effort to promote the first phase of the pastoral plan.

You were invited as leaders in various ministries which carry on the Church's primary mission of teaching the saving truths of the Gospel. It is our hope that the presentations and discussions of this workshop will help you to teach others the truths concerning human dignity and human rights.

Human dignity and human rights

The affirmation of the rights of God generates the affirmation of the rights of man. Truths about human dignity and rights are accessible to all, but in the Gospel we find the fullest expression and the strongest motive for commitment to their preservation and promotion.

Human dignity is rooted in the image and reflection of God in each of us. "God created man in his image; in the divine image he created him; male and female he created them" (Gn. 1:27). It was God who said: "Before I formed you in the womb I knew you, before you were born I dedicated you, a prophet to the nations I appointed you" (Jer. 1:5). It was God who said: "It is I who bring both death and life" (Dt. 32:39); "You shall not kill" (Ex. 20:13); "You must banish all shedding of innocent blood from among you if you mean to do what is right in the eyes of Yahweh" (Dt. 21:9); "He who sheds man's blood, shall have his blood shed by man, for in the image of God man was made" (Gn. 9:6).

For anyone who believes in God, human dignity, human rights and human life are inalienable and inviolable gifts from God, which must be preserved and defended. Deeply aware of these truths, the Catholic Church firmly believes that the promotion of human rights is required by the Scriptures and is central to her ministry. It is for this reason that the Catholic bishops of the United States, faithful to the Church's mission and ministry, issued the Pastoral Plan for Pro-Life Activities. It is a plan to promote the most basic of all human rights: the right to life, the right to be born.

Silence is concurrence and complicity

In his play, "The Deputy," Rolf Hochhuth accused the Pope of criminal silence. The communications media, including the *New York Times*, immediately criticized the hierarchy of the Catholic Church for its supposed failure to speak in defense of innocent human beings shipped to Nazi gas chambers.

Hochhuth's charges were soundly refuted by the Jewish historian Jeno Levai in his book, *The Church Did Not Keep Silent*; by the Israeli official Pinchas Lapide in his book, *Three Popes and the Jews*; by Dr. Joseph Lichten, a Polish Jew and head of the Intercultural Department of the Anti-Defamation League of B'Nai B'rith, and also by the eminent Philadelphia jurist, Dr. R.W. Kempner, the former United States Deputy Chief Prosecutor at the Nuremberg War Crimes Trials.

Some who severely criticized the Catholic hierarchy for its supposed failure to protest the killing of innocent human beings in Europe are now criticizing the Catholic hierarchy for protesting the killing of innocent human beings in the womb. Their tactics are familiar. They propagandize and headline what is considered the popular position on abortion. They try to create the impression that the pro-life stance is a minority position. And yet when the issue was placed before the public, the pro-life position was supported by a decisive majority. I refer to the referenda in Michigan and in North Dakota. Almost every time that this issue was submitted to State legislatures prior to the Supreme Court ruling, the vote was against abortion. Only when it was submitted to a minority group—the Supreme Court—was the vote, by split decision, in favor of abortion. Justice Blackman, who wrote the majority decision, was quoted as saying that the Court's abortion ruling "will be regarded as one of the worst mistakes in the Court's history or one of its greatest decisions." He did not seem to be sure. The fact is that in the 200 years of our history, no decision has had more disastrous implications for our stability as a civilized society.

The second tactic of the critics of the pro-life stance is to sabotage opponents by creating the impression that only a single religious denomination opposes abortion and tries to impose its moral code on others. Thus, in a January 11, 1969 editorial, the *New York Times* alleged: "Here, as elsewhere, the principal opponents of reform are the Catholic bishops, whose reservations have stood in the way of change for adherents of all other religions.... Abortion is a medical and legal, not a religious or political, matter."

The right to life is not an invention of the Catholic Church or of the Catholic hierarchy. Our Declaration of Independence affirms: "We hold these truths to be self-evident, that all men are created equal, that they are endowed by their Creator with certain inalienable rights, that among these are Life...." This right to life is affirmed in the United Nations Universal Declaration of Human Rights. The United Nations International Covenant on Civil and Political Rights declares: "Every human being has the inherent right to life. This right shall be protected by law.... Everyone shall have the right to recognition as a person before the law." The Declaration of the Rights of the Child, unanimously adopted by the United Nations General Assembly on November 20, 1959, declared that the child by reason of his physical and mental immaturity needs "special safeguards and care, including appropriate legal protection *before as well as after birth*." As Americans we subscribe to the right-to-life affirmations of our Declaration of Independence, and the affirmations of the United Nations. These documents are not the documents of the Catholic Church, but they are in accord with the teachings of the Catholic Church and of other Churches.

The old canard about imposing morality upon others is as absurd as it is impossible. All human beings are endowed by God with a free will, and all have the capacity to accept or reject the views of others. Either we all have the same right to speak out on public policy or no one has. We do not have to check our consciences at the door before we argue for what we think is best for society. As American citizens who are free to express our views, we can and must advocate positions which we believe will best serve the good of our country.

The *New York Times* statement that "Abortion is a medical and legal, not a religious or political, matter," articulates the Hitlerian principle that the State has absolute power over the life of an individual. In his euthanasia order, dated September 1, 1939, Hitler extended the responsibilities of the medical profession to exterminate the mentally and physically defectives. Hitler made extermination a medical and legal problem. Having started down this slope, it was an easy transition from mental and physical defectives to ailing concentration camp inmates, and from them to healthy but undesirable people, with the crescendo at Auschwitz and its Jews. To give medicine and law the sole autonomy in exterminating innocent life is precisely what occurred in Nazi Germany.

Whenever political judgment is separated from moral judgment, disorder and disaster follow. The right to life is not something sectarian, but a basic human right which must undergird any civilized society. It is for this reason that we who live in a free society and enjoy the freedom of speech must speak out — must shout in protest — against the principle of subordinating human life to the determination of the State, of individuals, or to medicine and law. We must protest the killing of innocent unborn life. We would be subject to the just criticism of history if we remained silent. In fact, our silence in a free society would not be tolerance, but concurrence and complicity in the crime of killing innocent life. We can and we must protest and we dare not be intimidated by unjust criticism of the advocates of abortion.

Continuing Holocaust

In recent weeks we have been reminded dramatically of man's inhumanity to man. The horror of the death of 29 million persons in World War II, the deliberate killing of 12 million

Jews, Catholics, Protestants and people of other faiths was brought to our attention, and many people asked how this could have happened.

The Holocaust is not an isolated event. The foundations for this horror were laid by materialistic, atheistic philosophies. These philosophies were expounded in the lecture halls of universities. They were expounded by Russian Nihilists. Karl Marx regarded the rights of man as a bourgeois illusion. He was hostile to the individualism which underlies the classical doctrine on human rights. He defended the principle that the State had unlimited legal rights over the individual.

Before the Holocaust occurred, millions of Armenians were massacred by the Turks. Hundreds of thousands of Ukrainians were executed by Russian Communists. In fact, the first victims of Hitler's mass-murder ethic were his own fellow Germans and Austrians. Upwards of 80,000, perhaps 100,000 countrymen — mentally ill, epileptics, feeble-minded and deformed — all unproductive, were killed without formality in the brand-new gas chambers, mostly in 1940-1941. After 1941, the gas chambers and the crematoria were dismantled and sent to the East. It was an easy transition from the wholesale extermination of the unproductives to the wholesale elimination of the *Untermenschen* — the undesirables. And since it was legally permissible to kill, the doctors took the opportunity for "scientific" experiments on healthy young Russians, Poles and Jews, men and women, boys and girls.

The Holocaust was not a single and isolated event in modern history. Recent articles by William F. Buckley, Jr., and William Safire in the *New York Times*, and an editorial in the *Catholic Standard and Times* all point to the fact that the torture and slaughter of innocents is continuing in our day. They point to the reports of Russian dissidents about the slave labor and concentration camps. They refer to the Nigerian genocidal war against the Ibo Tribes in the Biafran War. They point to the killing of tens of thousands of innocent people in Ruanda and Burundi. They mention the estimated three million Cambodians who have died as victims of Communism. Mr. Buckley wrote: "Right now in Cambodia, in proportion to the population of that country, more people are being killed and tortured than Jews under Hitler."

We can add that by the end of 1978, six million innocent, defenseiess, unborn children of all races, religions and nationalities will have been exterminated in an equally vicious attack against human life in our nation. The principle is the same: exterminate the unproductive, the undesirables, the unwanted.

It is an unalterable biological fact that every person comes into the world as a result of the genetic conjunction of two other persons. Medicine supports the fact that from conception, the child in its mother's womb is a distinct individual—an autonomous human being from the moment of fertilization, when the pattern of the individuality, constitutional development is irrevocably determined. The technique of "scapegoating" by declaring the unborn as not innocent and not human is not acceptable. If the unborn child is not human, what is it? If it is called a "potential human being," what is it in actuality? Various attempts to redefine "person," "human," and even "life" itself only reaffirm that the unborn is a human being.

Yes, the Holocaust continues, and it continues in our country. Just as Hitler, once he started down the slope that human life could be destroyed, could not stop short of the crematoria, so also, in our country, that slope which permitted the destruction of the child in the womb has been carried to the destruction of the live child outside the womb. Now there is a discussion about the destruction of the lives of defective and deformed children after birth, and the curtailment of life of the aged and gravely ill.

The Holocaust continues. We must speak out in protest and make every lawful effort to correct the horrendous mistake of the Supreme Court, and reaffirm that all human life is inviolable and is entitled to the protection of the law.

Deceptive euphemism

An editorial entitled "A New Ethic for Medicine and Society," in the September 1970 issue of *California Medicine*, noted: "The very considerable semantic gymnastics which are required to rationalize abortion as anything but the taking of human life would be ludicrous if not often put forth under socially impeccable auspices."

Pro-abortionists tend to use semantic gymnastics and deceptive and euphemistic language to disguise the reality that abortion is the killing of a human being.

The Planned Parenthood advocates of abortion have some difficulty explaining an answer in their 1963 pamphlet, "Plan Your Children for Health and Happiness." The answer given to the question: "Is birth control an abortion?" was "Definitely not. An abortion kills the life of a baby after it has begun. It is dangerous to your life and health. It may make you sterile so that when you want a child you cannot have it."

Pro-abortionists use the phrase, "Freedom to choose." To choose what? The death of an innocent human life? Is it a freedom to pass a death sentence on another? To be an executioner? Freedom of choice is not an absolute freedom. We do not have the freedom of choice to kill a person who offends us. A wife does not have the freedom of choice to kill her husband so that she can marry another. In fact, when it comes to paying taxes, obeying traffic laws, and even using foods and medicines not approved by the H.E.W., our freedom of choice is limited and even denied.

We hear the slogan that a woman has the right to control her own body. Control over her own body, indeed, but not at the expense of the life of another human being. If the inconvenience of the child in the womb justifies the killing of the child, what about the inconvenience caused by the child after birth, when the child's needs and demands are even greater?

The phrase "the right to privacy" is frequently used to explain abortion. The right to privacy is not explicitly mentioned in the Constitution. It was not considered a fundamental right. Even this nebulous right of privacy was qualified by the Supreme Court, when it declared that "the abortion decision is inherently and primarily a medical decision, and basic responsibility for it must rest with the physician." So in the first trimester, the woman's right to privacy is subject to the judgment of a physician. During the second trimester—when abortions are risky—the State may establish some guidelines to protect the health of the woman. In the third trimester, the State may establish laws to protect fetal life. The right to life is affirmed in the Declaration of Independence and in the Constitution. The right to privacy is not. Since either the doctor or the State has responsibility all during pregnancy, just how is the right to privacy actualized?

The expression to "terminate pregnancy" is a euphemism for abortion or the killing of human life.

The expression "reproductive freedom" must be labeled as deliberate deception. Abortion interferes with reproduction and in no way enhances reproductive freedom.

Pro-lifers are at times accused of being concerned only with a single issue. No one can be concerned about all the issues. We focus attention on the more or most important issues. Is there any issue more important than the right to life issue? Is there anything wrong in giving high priority to an all-important issue?

The allegation that the pro-life position is exclusively a Catholic position is an insult to the many non-Catholic people who are opposed to abortion. In every state, in every pro-life group, in the legislatures, non-Catholics are outstanding leaders in the fight for life. The referenda in Michigan and North Dakota, in which Catholics are in a minority, contradicts the allegation that the pro-life position is an exclusively Catholic position.

The Lord said to the prophet Ezekiel: "If I say to the wicked man, you shall surely die, and you do not warn him or speak out to dissuade him from his wicked conduct, the wicked man shall die for his sin, but I will hold you responsible for his death" (3:18).

We do have a responsibility. We must give testimony. We must be witnesses to the truth. The earliest post-scriptural documents of the Church, the Didache — Teaching of the Twelve Apostles — and the Epistle of Barnabas clearly state: "Do not kill a fetus by abortion or commit infanticide." Pope Sixtus V, in 1588, imposed an automatic excommunication for the actual destruction of a formed or unformed fetus. Pius IX eliminated the distinction between the animated and unanimated fetus. The teaching of the Church is clear: the right to life is a basic human right which should be protected by law, and abortion, the deliberate destruction of an unborn human being, is contrary to the law of God and is a morally evil act.

The Church's program of action in defense of life is not limited to prophetic denunciation. Our Holy Father, in his message to the United Nations on the 25th anniversary of the Universal Declaration of Human Rights, observed: "Mere denunciation, often too late or ineffective, is not sufficient. There must be an analysis of the deep-rooted causes of such situations and a firm commitment to face up to them and resolve them correctly."

It is a fact that some of the people who are shocked by the mass-murder ethic of this century unwittingly espouse the false principles which undergird such tragedies.

The first of these principles is the professed or practical denial of God. The true concept of human rights and human freedom is centered in God—not in man. Man cannot live without God. If he denies God, he will create his own gods. He will deify the individual, a race or a nation, and attribute to these divine authority. God is the ultimate and absolute value in life: the value to which all other values are referred, the one value which survives the collapse of all other values. The denial of God does not solve, but rather complicates and multiplies human problems. The denial of God was at the root of the problems which flowed from Marx's Communism and Hitler's National Socialism.

The second false principle denies that man is created to the image and likeness of God and that God gives man inalienable rights which the

State must respect and protect. The State is not the source of human rights and human freedom. The State is not omnipotent and does not have the ultimate authority over human life.

The third false principle is that which tends to qualify human life by such phrases as "potential or viable human life," as defective, unproductive or unwanted human life. All human life, from the moment of conception to natural death, is a gift from God and must be defended and protected.

It is sometimes alleged that the Church is a one-issue Church, focusing exclusively on the right to life. Actually the Church is involved in a multi-faceted ministry to human life. In its family life ministry, it emphasizes the importance of the family as the foundation of a healthy society. It is in the family that the individual lives and learns to balance personal rights with the rights of others. It is in the family that one learns to live as a brother or sister in the one family of God. It is in the family that one learns to respect all human life.

In its ministry and apostolate of education, the Church insists that God, the supreme factor in human life, must also be the supreme factor in education. How can a student learn the basic value of human life and respect human life if he does not know God and does not recognize the creative activity of God? If the child is taught that human life is a mere product of a biological function, with no intervention of God, then the child will regard a human being as tissue, protoplasm, as a non-person.

The Church has always been a leader in defending human life, human dignity and human rights. This inalienable fact is in a way recognized by those who allege incorrectly, of course, that it is the Catholic Church alone that opposes abortion. The Church's main contribution to the realization of human rights consists in a continuous and eminently practical process of education of her own members and through them the members of the entire community.

The Church also carries on a broad and practical ministry to human life in her social services and charities ministry. She takes care of the poor people on skid row, the retarded, the brain-damaged, the aged, the sick and handicapped and needy persons. She carries on a special ministry to youth during and after school. The Church certainly is not a one-ministry or a one-issue Church.

In their statement on *Human Life in Our Day*, the American Bishops stated: "We honor God when we reverence human life. When human life is served, man is enriched and God is acknowledged. When human life is threatened, man is diminished and God is less manifest in our midst."

Our faith calls us to serve human life. Our service, being human, is not always adequate, not always perfect, and our methods are not always as productive as we wish them to be. However, we are certain of the foundation of our commitment that "God, the Lord of Life, has conferred upon us the surpassing ministry of safeguarding human life, a ministry which must be fulfilled in a manner that is worthy of man."

I pray that this workshop may be a source of information and inspiration. I pray that we may resolutely pursue the ministry of safeguarding life, and never be deterred by the criticism of those who would inhibit our ministry. I pray that we may be dedicated to the ministry of improving and enhancing human life, so that we may achieve the fullness of life, both in time and in eternity.

Prayers for Our Nation and the World

A Prayer for Guidance

Invocation at Independence Hall, on July 4, 1962.

Almighty God, we Your children, assembled at this shrine of our nation's birth and symbol of its liberty, unite with our Founding Fathers in acknowledging You as the Source of all life, and the Author of all human rights and liberty.

Help us to appreciate that the Declaration of Independence is also a public profession of faith in You, and complete dependence upon You.

Help us to realize that Your precious gift of freedom may not be used to ignore You, disobey Your laws or to deny Your very existence.

We beg You for guidance, wisdom and courage to preserve the secure foundation of our freedom — Your divine authority. Bless the President and legislators and the judges of our nation, and preserve us from all evil. Amen.

A Prayer for Legislators and Judges

Invocation at the 175th Anniversary of the U.S. Constitution, Independence Hall, on September 17, 1962.

Almighty God, Creator and Ruler of the universe, Source of all human life, authority and liberty, we, Your grateful creatures, have assembled this day, at the venerated symbol of our nation's liberty and the shrine of our nation's birth, to commemorate the 175th anniversary of the adoption of the Constitution of our country.

Just as Washington opened the Constitutional Convention with the affirmation that "the event is in the hands of God," and our Founding Fathers proclaimed the religious foundations of all laws and of liberty, we also acknowledge You as the Master of life and of all human rights; we glorify You in Your works, and give thanks for the many blessings bestowed upon our beloved country and its people.

We beseech You, grant us a keen appreciation of our spiritual destiny, our dependence upon You, and responsibility to You as our final Judge. Broaden our visions so that the horizons of our life will extend beyond the grave.

We beg You, O Lord, for God-loving and God-fearing legislators and judges. Grant them the wisdom to understand current needs, and the discretion and courage to insure the continuity of the Constitution by interpreting and adapting it to modern circumstances, which are so vastly different from those which existed in

Constitutional days. Help them to avoid the narrow and inflexible interpretation, which may cause the Constitution to impinge upon the essential rights which it was designed to preserve.

Implant in our hearts a spirit of fraternal love, respect and understanding for all peoples of the earth, and eliminate all trace of suspicion, prejudice and hate.

Help us devote our talents and energy to the improvement of the well-being of the people of our nation and of the entire human race. Bless us, O Lord, and preserve us from all evil. Amen.

A Prayer for Courage, Faith and Hope

Invocation at the 20th Annual Convention American Veterans of World War II, on August 27, 1964.

Most merciful Father, we Your humble servants ask Your blessing. We beg mercy for the brave souls who died in conflict so that we may live in peace. Grant to them eternal rest, and to us a prayerful remembrance of them.

Share with us that love and concern for all men without exception to color, race or nation, which impelled Your Son to lay down His life for the salvation of all men.

Preserve in us that spirit of service and dedication to our country, so that we be as ready to work for the preservation, as we were ready to die in defense, of its life. Extend our interest and concern beyond our national boundaries to all the peoples of the family of nations.

Grant us the wisdom to appreciate that we are all soldiers in Your spiritual kingdom, committed to fight against the powers of darkness, against injustice, enslavement, treachery, deceit, greed, lust and all forms of immorality and evil.

Help us to march forward, through this vale of tears, resolute in courage, firm in faith and strong in hope. Lead us to our heavenly Jerusalem, where, free from warfare, sorrow and mourning, we shall enjoy, with all Your children, blessed and eternal peace, through the merits of Jesus Christ our Lord. Amen.

A Prayer To Secure Our God-given Rights

Benediction at the Republican National Convention, Miami, on August 23, 1972.

Lord God, Creator and Ruler of the universe, we acknowledge our dependence upon You as the Source, continued support and ultimate goal of life. With sincere repentance, we acknowledge and beg forgiveness for our faults and failures. We implore Your guidance, Your help and Your blessings.

The historical record of our nation constantly affirms that our republic was conceived and survives only on moral and religious foundations. The Declaration of Independence appealed to the self-evident principle that all men equally are creatures of God, endowed by Him with inalienable rights which governments must insure. The deep belief of the Founding Fathers in God, and their firm reliance upon His providence — epitomized in Lincoln's immortal words, "This nation under God" — was reaffirmed more precisely in the words of the Supreme Court: "We are a religious people whose institutions presuppose a Supreme Being." We salute our national flag, acknowledging that we are "under God," and our coins and currency proclaim that "In God we trust."

Just as all presidents acknowledged the religious heritage of our republic, so also President Eisenhower averred: "Without God, there could be no American form of government — nor an American way of life. Each day, we must ask Almighty God to keep His protecting hand over us so that we may transmit to those who come after us the heritage of a free people, secure in their God-given rights...."

In this hallowed tradition we ask You, Lord, to extend Your protecting hand over all who hold and seek public office. Shield them from all danger. Inspire them with courage to serve all the people — not as masters, but as stewards, accountable to You and to Your people. Help them to regulate their conduct by the unchanging principles of Your commandments. Let no fear of unjust criticism deter their efforts to serve this nation and the family of nations, particularly in pursuing the elusive goals of peace and justice.

Hear our prayer in behalf of all government officials, so that in exercising the authority which derives from You, they may please You and Your people, and together with them merit the promised eternal reward.

Bless them, bless all participants, viewers and listeners of this convention, and preserve us all from evil. Amen.

A Prayer for a Reawakening of Moral Sensitivity

Invocation at Carpenter's Hall, September 5, 1974 — Reconvening the First Continental Congress — 200th Anniversary.

(The opening ceremony was followed by speeches of thirteen Governors of the thirteen original states.)

"Almighty God, Creator and Ruler of the universe, we Your creatures assemble this morning to commemorate the First Continental Congress which opened on this site, this day and this hour two hundred years ago.

Our commemoration of this historic event includes a rededication and recommitment to the fundamental principles which inspired the Declaration of Rights, issued by the Congress and which were affirmed in the Declaration of Independence, the Constitution, and the Bill of Rights.

The fundamental principle underlying the Acts of the Congress and our governmental philosophy is that the spiritual is supreme; that man is of divine origin; that man possesses inalienable rights solely by reason of endowment by his Creator. This fundamental religious basis of our governmental philosophy is the foundation of a moral code which assumes that each individual is a creature of God and has a duty to obey God's law; that there are moral rights which are inalienable, because there are moral obligations which are unavoidable—to be fulfilled by all persons, at all times, and in all places.

A genuine recommitment to the fundamental principles underlying the acts of the Continental Congress calls for a reawakening of moral sensitivity, based on a profound conviction that we are one nation under God; that our form of government was conceived in and must survive on moral and religious foundations.

Our Founding Fathers expressed the firm conviction that the "superintending hand of Providence"—"the finger of God"—guided the formulation of the principles underlying our form of government, which came into existence, "influenced, guided, and governed by that omnipresent and beneficent Ruler, in whom all inferior spirits live and move and have their being" (Charles Pinckney, Hamilton, and Franklin).

As we rededicate ourselves to moral and religious foundations, we pray that all our government officials acquire a deeper appreciation of these foundations, and a deeper respect for the dignity and the divine destiny of every individual, of every human being.

Bless, O Lord, all participants in this commemorative event. Enlighten us all to acquire a deeper appreciation of the moral and religious principles which are the basis of our governmental philosophy, and help us all to conform to Your divine will and law. Amen.

A Prayer To Understand Our Starving Brothers

Invocation on the occasion of the opening of the Symposium on World Hunger, on February 11, 1975.

O Almighty God, Lord of creation and Father of us all, You assigned to man the task of subduing the earth, and because of his sin, man must earn his bread through toil and struggle. There are those of our brothers who have been lost in the struggle, who have no bread to fill their hunger or water to quench their thirst.

As we seek to understand the problem of man's hunger, give us the light to realize that scarcity does not dissolve our moral responsibility. Rather, it intensifies the nature of the moral choices we make. Expand the limits of our understanding of social justice to embrace knowing how to share, since the choices we make, as individuals and a nation, can mean the difference of life and death for others.

As the call of Lent summons us to penance and mortification, quicken our hearts by the outpouring of Your grace to prayer, fasting, and almsgiving. Let our response to our starving brothers spring from the depth of our faith to touch and inspire the charity of others.

While we labor to enhance the dignity of man and work that each man might live in accord with that God-given dignity, may we surrender all of our faculties to Your service, Lord, so that in working for our fellow man, it may be You working for them, using us as the instruments of Your labor.

Sustain us in our efforts. Give us the vision that comes from a strong faith, a perseverance rooted in hope, and a love which is an extension of Your own. We ask all this through Jesus Christ our Lord. Amen.

A Prayer for Social Justice and Charity

Invocation for the 67th Annual Convention of the Tile Contractors' Association of America, on October 6, 1975.

God, the Father of all men, we implore Your graces and blessings upon all participants in this 67th Annual Convention of the Tile Contractors' Association of America.

As we open this Convention, we acknowledge You as our Creator, the Master of all life and the source of all our blessings. We give You thanks for the many blessings—especially the blessings of freedom—bestowed upon our beloved country and its people. We dedicate this Convention to Your greater honor and glory, and humbly implore Your guidance and assistance in our deliberations and decisions.

We pray for a clear understanding and application of the principle that the earth, though divided among private owners, must provide for the needs of all men, and that private ownership and free enterprise cannot be pursued to the detriment of other individuals or of the common good. Help us to appreciate that man is but a steward of his possessions, with definite responsibilities of justice and charity towards his fellow men, and that ultimately every man will be called to give You an account of his stewardship.

Help us to promote our own best interests on the constructive principle of social and moral unity and to avoid the destructive principles of sordid selfishness, rigorous individualism, and ruthless competition. Help us to remember that our own best interests and the best interests of all men will be served best by mutual cooperation for the sake of social justice and charity.

Hear our prayer, O Lord, that under Your guidance and inspiration our deliberations and decisions will promote Your holy will and the best interests of all men.

A Prayer for the Common Good

Invocation at the Inauguration of Mayor Rizzo and the Induction of Members of City Council, of the Judiciary and other elected officials, on January 6, 1976.

Almighty God, Father of all men, Source of all authority, we ask Your blessings on the Honorable Mayor, members of the City Council and of the Judiciary and all elected officials as they assume the responsibility of the offices entrusted to them.

In this first week of our Bicentennial year, we give You thanks for the countless blessings bestowed on our nation since its birth in this city of Philadelphia, and upon this city and its citizens.

We pray for all who are elected or appointed to offices of stewardship and authority. May their efforts to exercise authority and meet the obligations of their office, reflect:

— A candor and truthfulness that inspire trust.

— A stewardship which husbands public resources and imposes burdens on struggling citizens only when inevitable, and only with reluctance.

— A faithfulness to a public trust, free of lust for power, popularity or personal profit.

— A greater commitment to public benefit than to political loyalty.

— A conviction that "We are a religious people" — "One nation under God" — which publicly proclaims, "In God We Trust."

— A sense of accountability to their constituents and also to their Creator, who will be their all-knowing Judge.

Grant them vision to perceive current needs, and courage and discretion to meet them.

Grant them the wisdom to respond to the pleas of the poor, the unemployed and the disadvantaged.

Grant that as the eyes of the nation focus this year on Philadelphia, they might find in every act of these officials the selfless dedication which marked the beginnings of our nation: a fierce dedication to human dignity and human liberty, blended with a deep concern for the common good.

May the pursuit of life, liberty and happiness inspire their deliberations and be the test of all their decisions.

Shower Your blessings on all here assembled. Help us to appreciate that the brotherhood of man which we strive to promote cannot be actualized unless we acknowledge You as our common Father. Help us in this year of grace, the Bicentennial year, to render You honor and glory, and to radiate Your all-embracing love. Amen.

A Prayer for a New Birth of Freedom Under God

Invocation at the Bicentennial Conference on Religious Liberty, on April 29, 1976.

Almighty Father, we stand in reverent awe before the works of Your creation — the beauty of the universe and the marvel of man, "whom you have made a little less than a god and crowned with glory and honor" (Ps. 8). You have given man power over the works of Your hands and have asked that he use the precious gifts of his intelligence and freedom to help fashion a world that acknowledges You as its beginning and its final destiny.

As we conclude this National Bicentennial Conference on Religious Liberty, we beg Your grace that we may work more diligently toward that day when the whole of creation "will be set free from its bondage and obtain the glorious liberty of the children of God" (Rom. 8); that we may strive more faithfully toward that vision which sees "neither Jew nor Greek, slave nor free" (Gal. 3:28) and acknowledges the brotherhood of man as a necessary consequence of the Fatherhood of God; that we may look toward that new heaven and new earth where God Himself will be with His people and where all things will be made new (Rv. 21:4-5).

Let all men realize that the exercise of their religious freedom is the source of their responsibility to work for the common good of all. Assist our efforts to that end with Your power, so that this nation which was conceived in liberty and dedicated to human freedom and equality might experience a *new* birth of freedom under God, whose Fatherhood excludes national, social, racial or economic distinctions.

May Your kingdom come and Your will be done—on earth as it is in heaven. Amen.

A Prayer for the Right to Life

Benediction at the Semi-Annual Meeting—Pennsylvania Conference of State Trial Judges, on March 25, 1977.

Lord God, we thank You for this opportunity to share and to renew our commitment to the sound administration of justice. For the inspiring words and the challenges to our responsibilities, we are grateful.

We rejoice that the cornerstone of our philosophy of government is belief in God; that our concept of freedom is centered in You — God — not in man alone; that explicit in the principle and practice of this one nation under God is the recognition of You, God, as the origin of human existence and dignity, the Source of our inalienable rights, the ultimate authority in life, the destiny of our aspirations and the final Judge of our thoughts, words and deeds.

We pledge our dedication to the concept that the primary object of our concern is the human person rather than the State, and that the American system of jurisprudence must remain the bastion of the human right to life at every stage and condition and of responsible freedom to pursue life's potential.

A Prayer To Safeguard Our Sacred Rights

Invocation at Valley Forge National Historical Park, on December 19, 1977, at the Commemoration of the 200th Anniversary of the arrival of George Washington's Army at Valley Forge for the 6-month winter encampment, and for the Naturalization Ceremony for 200 new citizens.

Almighty God, we acknowledge You as the Creator and Ruler of the universe, and as the Source of our dignity, our rights, our freedom and liberty.

As we conclude this ceremony commemorating the 200th anniversary of the arrival of Washington's army at Valley Forge, and complement it with the naturalization of 200 new citizens, we thank You for the faith of the Continental Congress in the "immutable laws of nature and of nature's God."

We thank You for the courage and determination of the poorly clad and unbooted rebel army of ragtag quality, which through its encampment at this place became a "skilled force" which gained victory and the blessings of freedom which succeeding generations have enjoyed and which we enjoy today—a freedom which is regrettably not enjoyed by people in many parts of the world.

We pray that this faith in You, and the courage and determination of the rebel army may permeate the diverse people which comprise our nation—a diversity reflected in the 200 new citizens. Our nation, now as then, is bedeviled with problems and burdened with challenges, but our nation, now as then, has great strength and magnificent promise. May Your guidance and the spirit of Valley Forge make us worthy of the sacrifices of those who fought for our freedom.

May this ceremony be an occasion of rededication to the spirit and efforts which gave birth to our nation. May the principles of liberty and justice for all, and our safeguard of the sacred right to life and to religious freedom, be the hallmarks of our citizenship. May we never forget Washington's admonition that religion and morality are the indispensable supports of our government and that morality cannot be maintained without religion.

May we ever be conscious of our individual and national dependence upon and responsibility to You. May Your blessings descend upon and remain with all the participants in this ceremony and upon all the peoples in our nation. Amen.

A prayer to renew our society

Invocation at the City Council Meeting, Philadelphia, Pa., on August 10, 1978. The Council presented the Cardinal with a Resolution on the occasion of the death of Pope Paul VI.

God, our Father, we acknowledge You as the Creator and Master of the universe. We, your creatures, need Your guidance and assistance. On behalf of this City Council of Philadelphia, we beg the gifts of wisdom and decision in difficulties and emergencies; discretion and reserve in the intimacies of their relations with all citizens. Help them to be firm without being harsh, faithful without being slavish, accurate without being mechanical, and let no striving after perfection or organization or after skill in method or treatment overlook that personal and ardent love which must permeate all our service to Your people in this City of Brotherly Love.

Send the healing power of Your love upon the people and government of this city, which in the past days has experienced so sad and tragic an ending to a strange and bizzare chapter in our history.

Help us to understand that our weak human nature, unaided by Your grace, cannot renew society, cannot lead to peace, cannot reduce violence, nor quench the passion of hatreds which produce divisions. As we strive for justice and condemn injustice and sin, we must embrace the weak, the misguided, and even the senseless and radical with Your love. We cannot react with hatred or with violence.

At the same time, help us to develop in all a respect for Your law and commandments which bring order, and which enable all of us to live as brothers and sisters in this City of Brotherly Love.

Help the members of this Council; inspire and guide them to live up to the highest and noblest responsibilities of their office.

Daughters of St. Paul

IN MASSACHUSETTS
    50 St. Paul's Avenue, Boston, Ma. 02130
    172 Tremont Street, Boston, Ma. 02111
IN NEW YORK
    78 Fort Place, Staten Island, N.Y. 10301
    59 East 43rd St., New York, N.Y. 10017
    625 East 187th Street, Bronx, N.Y. 10458
    525 Main Street, Buffalo, N.Y. 14203
IN NEW JERSEY
    Hudson Mall — Route 440 and
        Communipaw Ave., Jersey City, N.J. 07304
IN CONNECTICUT
    202 Fairfield Avenue, Bridgeport, Ct. 06604
IN OHIO
    2105 Ontario St. (at Prospect Ave.), Clevelahd, Oh. 44115
    25 E. Eighth Street, Cincinnati, Oh. 45202
IN PENNSYLVANIA
    1719 Chestnut St., Philadelphia, Pa. 19103
IN FLORIDA
    2700 Biscayne Blvd., Miami, Fl. 33137
IN LOUISIANA
    4403 Veterans Memorial Blvd., Metairie, La. 70002
    1800 South Acadian Thruway, P.O. Box 2028,
        Baton Rouge, La. 70802
IN MISSOURI
    1001 Pine St. (at North 10th), St. Louis, Mo. 63101
IN TEXAS
    114 East Main Plaza, San Antonio, Tx. 78205
IN CALIFORNIA
    1570 Fifth Avenue, San Diego, Ca. 92101
    46 Geary Street, San Francisco, Ca. 94108
IN HAWAII
    1143 Bishop St., Honolulu, Hi. 96813
IN ALASKA
    750 West 5th Avenue, Anchorage, Ak. 99501
IN CANADA
    3022 Dufferin Street, Toronto 395, Ontario, Canada
IN ENGLAND
    57, Kensington Church Street, London W. 8, England
IN AUSTRALIA
    58, Abbotsford Rd., Homebush, N.S.W., Sydney 2140,
    Australia